Praise for He Still Speaks

There is no other book that I am aware of that so thoroughly and inspirationally deals with the subject of New Covenant prophecy. I have known and walked with both Wayne and Tom for 25 years and can testify to their integrity and gifting in the ministry of the prophetic. As a pastor I have hosted "Prophetic Presbyteries" regularly for more than 20 years and nothing we do has more positive impact in the lives of our leaders. This book takes one behind the scenes of the prophetic and provides the theology and inspiration behind it. God is still speaking and what He has to say needs to be heard! This book is a must read for anyone interested in a biblical and practical application of this spiritual gift.

Clark Whitten
Senior Pastor
Grace Church, Orlando, Florida

What the Church so desperately needs right now is dynamic words directly from God. We, the Church, are given the highest calling of making the invisible kingdom of God visible to the world. Tom Lane and Wayne Drain have practically and biblically presented the incredible value of prophetic ministry inside the four walls of the Church along with highlighting how it can expose the unchurched to the love of God. I believe He Still Speaks *is a NOW message for the Church, and I believe if you read this book, you'll not only be encouraged to hear God more regularly yourself, you'll also be encouraged to start telling others what God is speaking to you in a way that will honor God and help them.*

Christine Caine
Director of Equip and Empower Ministries / Founder of The A21 Campaign
Sydney, Australia / Los Angeles, California

God's Word encourages us to test prophetic words. Because of their fruit, this qualifies Wayne and Tom to teach on the subject out of a far-ranging foundation of respect from those who have received prophetic words these two men have given. I found this book to be inspiring, practical and important. God has especially used Wayne to bring His word to many of the UK's leaders and Levites. And you can see the fruit of his ministry in the songs and lives of those God has used to bless the church worldwide ... true fruit from true prophets.

Les Moir
A&R Director of Kingsway and Integrity Music
Eastbourne, England

Tom Lane and Wayne Drain remove the mystery and the fear that many of us experience when coming into the presence of prophets and prophecy. Pointing to scriptures again and again to explain the prophetic, this book lays out exactly why prophecy is given, the importance of prophecy and the danger to be found in its misuse. An everyman's guide to understanding the prophetic, packed full of explanations and examples, this is by far one of the most practical, easy to read and easy to understand books written on this subject.

John Paculabo
Managing Director of Global Song Development
at Kingsway and Integrity Music
Eastbourne, England

Presbytery has changed my life and our church. Tom Lane and Wayne Drain are dear friends and have led presbytery services in our church many times. They are men of character and are highly qualified to write this book. As seasoned pastors, Tom and Wayne write from the perspective of those in love with the Church and with the highest regard for prophetic propriety. I highly recommend this book to anyone interested in growing in the gift of the prophetic and implementing presbytery into the life of your church.

Jimmy Evans
Senior Elder of Trinity Fellowship Church
Amarillo, Texas

He Still Speaks *is a book rooted in Scripture with loads of practical stories and lessons that need to be read by those who want to believe God speaks today. God has much to say to individuals, communities and nations. This book will help develop a mature and sensible approach to the prophetic. It is both pastoral and prophetic—a most unusual mix.*

Gerald Coates
Founder of Pioneer / Speaker / Author / Broadcaster
London, England

*I am so thankful Tom and Wayne wrote this book, but I am more grateful that God does indeed **still** speak to us. It is possible to hear His voice and encourage others along the way. I pray this book awakens all of us to know God personally and to hear Him clearly.*

Brady Boyd
Senior Pastor of New Life Church / Author of *Sons and Daughters*
Colorado Springs, Colorado

Wayne and I have been friends and worked together for more than 25 years. I have seen him operate with great integrity in his prophetic gifting, and my family and I have benefitted greatly from the words of prophecy he has given us. Wayne and Tom's book will help many understand the role of prophecy within the everyday life of the Body of Christ.

Noel Richards
Singer / Songwriter
Palma, Spain

As you read the pages of this book, you will be energized to want more of God. You will also be refreshed as you turn each page. The reason why is this is written by two guys who don't just have some ideas about prophecy ... they have lived *in embracing the prophetic today. This is a brilliant book! I recommend it to pastors, small group leaders and church members. Get your hands on a copy of this!*

Paul Weston
Pastor of New Generation Church / Spring Harvest Event Leadership Team
London, England

The role of prophetic ministry in the local church is vitally important. Many of us have been put off by some of the excesses and abuses of this ministry or we've never seen the true gift modelled effectively. Wayne and Tom write from their years of experience as church leaders. They outline a way to operate in the prophetic so you can do all this amazing gift is intended to—mature disciples and encourage believers to confidently and fully be who God has called them to be. I highly recommend this book!

Billy Kennedy
Leader of Pioneer
London, England

Still HE SPEAKS

EMBRACING THE PROPHETIC TODAY

WAYNE DRAIN & TOM LANE

GATEWAY®
PUBLISHING

While the authors make every effort to provide accurate URLs for external or third-party Internet websites at the time of printing, neither they nor the publisher assume any responsibility for changes or errors made after publication.

Some names and details of actual events have been changed to protect the identities of the persons involved.

Editorial Director Stacy Burnett
Senior Editor S. George Thomas
Editor Joyce Freeman
Art Director Shane Dennehey
Cover Design Melissa Runyon
Layout Katrina Sirmon

Gateway Press, an imprint of Gateway Publishing
700 Blessed Way
Southlake, TX 76092
GatewayPublishing.com

Printed in the United States of America.

To June—my wife and best friend.
Your love and support means more to me than I
could ever adequately express ... but I'll keep trying.

To my wonderful mom who "prayed me in"
to God's service and to my dad who is now leaning
over the portals of heaven spurring me on.

To Fellowship of Christians—my community of faith—
and our wonderful Elder Team. I have been privileged
to serve as your pastor all these years. David, Chris,
Tim, Greg and Travis—you're the best!

Wayne

To Jan, my wife and partner in ministry and life
for over 40 years. Your influence in my life has been
more than you know, but one day you will fully know
because God will reveal how critical your role
has been in His work through us!

To each of my children and their spouses:
Todd and Blynda Lane; Braxton and Lisa Corley;
Tyler and Marci Lane; and Brett and Lindsay Huckins.
Your love for me and commitment to God brings joy to my life
and lays a foundation for God's work through my life
and our family. Thank you for being tender to God
and faithful to our love for Him.

To the Gateway Church congregation, leadership
and all those who open their hearts to hear, believe
and obey God in their service to Him and others!

Tom

To my spiritual father, Lattie McDonough. Thank you for your encouragement and unfailing faith in me. This book would not have been written without your many investments in me through the years.

To my close friends and family whose support has been so generous: Kenny and Lindsey Drain; Tim and Rhonda Drain; Mark and Laura Gotcher; Phil Love; Bobby and Kim Adams; Steve and Jane Galbo; Scott and Bethany Palmer; Kent and Laine Fancher; Chris and Jan Horan; and Mack and Sherri Streety.

To my ministry pals around the world who inspired and encouraged me: Tom Lane; Clark Whitten; Robert Morris; Brady Boyd; Jimmy Evans; Bill and Debra Leckie; Noel and Tricia Richards; Brian and Pauline Houston; Les Moir; Billy Kennedy; Olen Griffing; Gerald Coates; John Paculabo; Steve Pyle; David and Dale Garratt; Dave and Rhian Day; Pete and Linda Lyne; Graham Perrins; and Paul Weston.

And last but not least, to my family who encouraged me to write down the stories: June; Chris and Mary Ann; Esther and Ben; Rhian and Jasen; Blake; Madison; and Kenzie. I love you so much!

Wayne

To my best friend Jimmy Evans. You saw God's purpose in me and encouraged me to reach for it. In so many incredible ways, your friendship and influence have been a rich gift from God. You challenged me to ask God for His prophetic words to be revealed through my life and supported me as I learned to hear God and minister. Thank you!

To Pastor Robert Morris and my friends who are the Elders, Senior Team and staff of Gateway Church. Robert, you challenged me in prophetic ministry and mentored me in prophetic presbytery. Thank you for your friendship and your leadership. I feel so honored to serve with the awesome men and women who make up the leadership of Gateway Church. Thank you for challenging me in love and service to God and others!

To those who have believed in me and have walked with me on my journey in ministry: Larry Titus, Jimmy Evans, Robert Morris, Clark Whitten and David Smith.

Finally, to my friend and partner in this project, Wayne Drain. Without your encouragement and drive, this project would still be a Word document outline on my laptop. Thank you, my friend!

Tom

Special thanks to the Create Publishing team. To Thomas Miller and David Smith who have encouraged and supported this project. To S. George Thomas, Stacy Burnett and Joyce Freeman who edited the entire book and worked tirelessly to make this become a reality. Finally, to Tia Bowen, Stephanie Buchanan, Lawrence Swicegood and the Gateway Design team who make all things come to life ... you are amazing in your service and creativity.

Wayne and Tom

Foreword

I was saved in 1981, and my first personal experience with prophetic ministry happened two years later when a group of men came to the church I was attending to do a prophetic presbytery. At the time, I had no idea what a prophetic presbytery was, but since my pastor invited me to attend one of the meetings, I decided to go. On Thursday morning, Debbie and I went to the service, and my pastor said, "There's a young couple in our church whom I want to call up front." The team doing the presbytery didn't know who I was or what I did ... they didn't know *anything* about me, and my pastor didn't tell them anything. The team started prophesying over me about traveling to the nations and preaching and doing evangelism, and ultimately, even writing and pastoring ... all of the things I do today! It was an amazing event in my life with the Lord, and it happened through a prophetic presbytery.

They went on to prophesy that one day I would do prophetic presbyteries! The thought of walking up to people I didn't know and prophesying about their gifts and callings was terrifying. I remember thinking, "I could *never* do this."

However, I eventually had the privilege of traveling with several spiritual mothers and fathers who mentored and taught me about prophecy. The first time I had the chance to go and minister with these spiritual mentors (who have since gone on to be with the Lord), I couldn't wait to prophesy over someone. The first couple came up, and I was ready. But my mentors told me to wait. Then, the second couple came forward. I was again told to wait. Then the third couple ... then the fourth ... and so on it went for a while. Finally, one of the men turned to me and said: "Okay, Robert, it's your turn now." But this time, I didn't have anything to say!

And then suddenly, a thought popped into my head. I went forward and began to speak that thought by faith. As I spoke, the thought grew. It was so strong and so right on that people began to cry. Seeing their reaction to hearing God speak something to them that no one else knew was so encouraging. I called my wife, Debbie, that night and told her: "This is what I was born to do!"

After that experience, I started traveling and doing prophetic presbyteries in churches. One of the churches I was invited to come and do a presbytery for was Wayne Drain's church (this was more than 20 years ago). Not long before, the Lord gave me a life scripture during my quiet time He said was specifically for me. I didn't tell anyone about this scripture ... not even Debbie. That evening at Wayne's church, a group of people gathered around and began to pray, bless and encourage me. That's when Wayne stepped forward and said: "I have a word from the Lord for you, Robert." He began to prophesy: "Have not I recently given you a life scripture that you have not even told your wife about?" He then went on to actually quote the scripture the Lord had given me. I remember thinking to myself: *It's possible this man is a prophet!* To this day, that word is one of the most accurate prophecies I have ever received. I have known Wayne for over 25 years now. He has ministered at all of Gateway's prophetic presbyteries—every one of them! I can say without reservation that Wayne truly has the heart of a pastor and the wisdom to help other pastors understand prophetic church ministry.

Some years later, when my friend Tom Lane was at Trinity Fellowship, I mentioned to him that he needed to come with me to a prophetic presbytery and see what it's all about. So Tom, along with Jimmy Evans, Clark Whitten and David Smith, came with me to a prophetic meeting where Tom and Jimmy were prophesied over. After that, Tom began to develop a hunger for prophetic ministry and began to really grow in this area. Since coming to Gateway, Tom has taken on the responsibility of helping other churches learn about prophetic ministry and how to operate in it in a balanced and scriptural way.

Throughout my years in ministry, I've come to the realization that people are truly hungry for the prophetic. As local church leaders, we cannot afford to ignore it, avoid it, despise it or treat it with contempt (1 Thessalonians 5:19–21). The gift of prophecy is one of the gifts of the Holy Spirit, and according to

1 Corinthians 14:3, its primary purpose is to exhort, edify and comfort us. Another reason why prophetic ministry is absolutely vital is it allows people to hear God in a safe and healthy environment and for God to encourage and confirm to them what He's called them to do.

We've held prophetic presbyteries from the very first years of Gateway, and it has been a stabilizing factor in our church that has produced life, health and some of the greatest fruit in individual's lives. I believe healthy prophetic ministry in the local church gives us a three-fold witness: God speaks to our hearts through His Word and Spirit, confirmation of the local leadership of that church and a prophetic confirmation. This is a threefold cord that is not easily broken.

Prophecy is an incredibly powerful gift and ministry, but if we don't provide healthy boundaries for it in our local churches, then things can get unbalanced and people will be spiritually abused. It's imperative for us as church leaders to make an effort to learn what God's Word says about this gift of the Spirit and then help our church understand and operate in it.

Because of this great need, I encouraged Wayne and Tom to write this book to help lay out guidelines for healthy prophetic ministry we have learned and implemented here at Gateway. Because of their wisdom, understanding and pastors' hearts, I believe with all of my heart that Wayne Drain and Tom Lane are two of the best men to help pastors and church leaders understand prophetic ministry. Through this book, I know you will be encouraged to identify and walk in the gifts and callings God has for you and your church.

Robert Morris
Founding Senior Pastor of Gateway Church
Author of *The Blessed Life*, *The Power of Your Words*
and *The God I Never Knew*

Contents

Why We Wrote This Book

TOM LANE

The Lord has used me to minister prophetically for more than 20 years. For most of those years, I traveled to churches where I wasn't on staff and ministered prophetically to the congregation and leaders. I usually ministered as part of a team and quite often did so with my friend and fellow pastor Wayne Drain.

A few years ago, Wayne and I were doing prophetic ministry together at a church. We were sitting in a hotel lobby before our evening service and talking about how prophetic ministry had impacted our lives and churches. We both marveled and were humbled by God's work in us and through us over the years.

That's when Wayne had an "aha" moment. He looked at me and said, "We ought to write a book together on prophetic ministry!" What's amazing about this is Wayne had no idea I had been thinking about writing on the prophetic for quite some time. I had even gone as far as preparing a rough outline of chapters and subjects I would address if I ever got around to writing the book!

In truth, it's a little intimidating to write on the prophetic for several reasons. While I agree with the theology of some who have written on the prophetic, their methodology is vastly different from what I've experienced, and I find it hard to relate to their perspective on prophetic ministry in the church. Then there are those I look up to who have ministered prophetically for years, and I would say they are way more seasoned than me and better qualified to write a book on the prophetic.

But when Wayne suggested we write together, my heart leaped. I immediately told him I was interested and showed him the work I had already begun. It turned out he had been doing some work on the subject too! We agreed to consider combining our efforts to produce a book sharing our perspective and experiences to further God's work in His Church. As Wayne and I have ministered prophetically in churches over the years, we've seen how it can build up the members and leaders of a church. And from our own experiences in our lives, we know firsthand its tremendous benefits.

Our desire is to present prophetic ministry to you in a biblically accurate way. You can rest easy knowing we're not heretics; we're just local church pastors who love God and His people. If you've seen people abuse prophecy before or if you believe the gift of prophecy has no place in the church today, we understand your caution. If you're confused or confounded by how prophecy can operate in a believer's life and the church in a life-giving way, our hope is this book will bring you clarity about the biblical methods of ministering prophetically. And if you've been hurt by prophetic ministry or by prophets, our prayer is these pages will bring healing to your spirit and heart and restore in you an anticipation of God's intimate, personal, miraculous work.

Before Wayne shares his perspective with you, I want to give you a little background about myself and my personal journey with the Lord. I'm a right-brain kind of guy. I love order and a logical approach to understanding things, and this is how I approach most things in my life. But as I've walked with God for more than 40 years, I've learned He is bigger, deeper and more complicated and intricate, yet also simpler than my logic and desire for order can fully grasp. When I received the Holy Spirit into my life, a new aspect of my journey with God began—one in which I've learned to trust more than I understand. I've learned to listen to simple impressions and train myself to discern the inner voice of God. Through the years, my relationship with God has become more personal and intimate while my love for Him has become deeper and stronger.

I was never personally hurt by prophecy, but the thought of others being hurt by its misuse or abuse caused me great concern. When I was younger, I viewed prophecy as being more about embarrassing correction and humiliation rather than loving affirmation, encouragement and comfort. And to some degree, that is precisely what I saw firsthand and heard from many people's accounts. So when a trusted pastor led me and a group of church leaders in an exercise of pressing in to God, listening to Him and speaking what He said to the group, I was intimidated and very cautious. From that first tentative beginning through many years of loving God and receiving from Him in a myriad of ways, I've repeatedly experienced God's encouragement, guidance and comfort through prophetic ministry. While prophetic ministry is just one of the ways God personally impacts our lives, it has been my experience that it has an awe-inspiring impact when it's done in a way that reflects the heart of God to His people.

As Wayne and I share our understanding of what the Bible has to say about the prophetic along with some practical guidance on how to incorporate it into church ministry, my prayer is you will be encouraged to know God is still speaking, and one of His life-giving methods of speaking is through prophecy. I hope you enjoy the read and are inspired to act!

WAYNE DRAIN

I became a Christian during the Jesus Movement of the early 1970s. At the time, I was excited about the chance to be involved with a God who's alive and communicates directly with people without always having to go through a middle man. That is still a huge factor for me today. I didn't buy into a religion or a set of rituals; I bought into a relationship. And there is healthy communication in healthy relationships.

In college, I served in student ministry as a worship leader, songwriter, recording artist, chair setter-upper, teacher and, as someone once described me, "a pastor with a prophetic edge." I enjoyed serving, but knew I couldn't continue doing everything I was doing for much longer. I was starting to receive words of knowledge, words of wisdom and prophetic words for people without fully understanding what they were about. I cried out to God for clarity and direction for my life. He answered with a

clear confirmation of my calling as a minister when three different people from three different nations gave the same prophetic
word over me within a few weeks of each other. That prophetic
word still rings in my spirit and serves to keep me focused to this
day: "You will lead a great church, and you will prophesy to the
nations." Those thirteen simple words clarified my course for
ministry and kept me from being drawn away from my areas of
gifting and calling. Those words gave me the courage to say yes or
no to various invitations to serve and minister. And for 40 years
now, I have led the same church and ministered in prophetic
ministry and worship leading in at least 35 nations.

When I first began to explore what the Scriptures say about
prophets, prophecy and presbyteries, I was amazed more wasn't
written about these wonderful avenues of service and ministry.
The things that had been written were for the most part fantas-
tic and sensational but seemed to only be reserved for the "super
ministers" who were in the vein of Old Testament prophets—big
on law and small on grace. However, there were some, like my
mentor Lattie McDonough and others, who were embracing
prophetic ministry from a New Testament perspective. Having
grown up in a very legalistic church, it seemed too good to be
true to believe prophetic ministry could be about encouragement, exhortation and comfort. As I explored, I was privileged
to meet other men and women in various parts of the world who
were rediscovering prophetic ministry that brought affirmation,
confirmation, life and joy. I observed people operating in the gifts
of the Spirit (1 Corinthians 12) while also exhibiting the fruits of
the Spirit (Galatians 5).

As I began to take steps of faith in my own journey, it was thrilling to see a positive impact on people who were receptive to prophetic ministry. Developing my gifts within a community of people
helped me explore the incredible gift of prophetic ministry while
enjoying the benefits of loving counsel and a spiritual covering.

Through the years, it has been a blessing to serve on various prophetic teams with men of integrity and character such
as my good friend Tom Lane. And it has been such a pleasure

to co-write this book with him. Our hope is these pages will be inspiring and helpful in practical ways to all who believe God is still speaking to people who are willing to listen. As pastors who prophesy, our desire is to see people built up and strengthened in their faith. And we want to see a new generation of pastors and prophets raised up to bless God's people. Most of all, we sincerely hope this book will serve those who read it to stay open to our God who is still speaking to those who have ears to hear.

Principles
of
Prophetic Ministry

1

EVERYONE NEEDS A WORD FROM GOD

Tom Lane

---

*Your word is a lamp to my feet
and a light to my path.*

Psalm 119:105 (NKJV)

Over the centuries, there have been some pretty crazy things done in the name of God ... the Crusades, the Salem Witch Trials, slavery ... to name just a few. And from the earliest days of the Church, there have been counterfeit imitations of what is godly and right—men with self-serving intentions and outright charlatans who sought to wreak destruction in people's lives for their own personal gain and glory rather than God's.

There is perhaps no ministry in the church with more glaring examples of excess and counterfeit expressions than in the area of prophetic ministry. It doesn't take much of a search to come across abuses and counterfeit manifestations or someone who has experienced or witnessed them firsthand. That being said, we must realize the counterfeit of anything never diminishes the real deal. And this is especially true of prophetic ministry. It is real, useful and very-much needed today.

There are many people who don't believe prophecy is a gift God bestows or believers need to actively use today. There are just as many others who see it solely as a rod of correction to expose and root out sin from the ranks of God's people.

We felt the need to write a book about the gift of prophecy and its use in the lives of people, because we firmly believe the role of prophetic ministry is as vital today as it ever has been in the church. The prophet Amos wrote, "Surely the Sovereign Lord *does nothing without revealing his plan to his servants the prophets*" (Amos 3:7, NIV; emphasis added). The Apostle Paul declared in his letter to the Corinthian church: "Pursue love, yet *desire earnestly spiritual gifts, but especially that you may prophesy*" (1 Corinthians 4:1, NASB; emphasis added). Paul went on to write this encouragement to the church at Thessalonica: "Do not quench the Spirit; *do not despise prophetic utterances*" (1 Thessalonians 5:19–20, NASB; emphasis added). And John wrote: *"the testimony of Jesus is the spirit of prophecy"* (Revelation 19:10, NASB; emphasis added). All these biblical commands lead us to some simple questions: Who among us doesn't want Jesus to be at work in His Church? Who among us doesn't need a word from God?

> **WE KNOW GOD SPEAKS TO US THROUGH THE BIBLE, BUT IS THERE NO NEW EXPRESSION OF GOD'S INFALLIBLE WORD BEING GIVEN TODAY?**

Your theology or experience may have led you to close the door on any contemporary expression of the Holy Spirit's work; however, there is an element of God's work in His Church and among His people that is incomplete without prophetic ministry.

As many Christians pursue a deeper, more intimate relationship with God, they come to the place in their seeking where they ask these questions: Is prophetic ministry still for today?

We know God speaks to us through the Bible, but is there no new expression of God's infallible word being given today? And what if our experience with prophetic ministry or gifts of the Spirit borders on the weird? Is it valid for today? How do I embrace it as an authentic and healthy expression of ministry in our church? Do all prophetic words have to be harsh and dominating? Does the Old Testament model of prophetic ministry really reflect the way God feels about His Church and His children today? Are we in rebellion if we question the revelation and application of a prophetic word? If we resist a prophet or his word, are we resisting God? These are all completely legitimate questions we must find answers to if we're going to allow and embrace prophetic expression in our lives and prophetic ministry in our churches.

When it comes to hearing a word from God, I have found most people feel like I did initially ... *fearful*. Although there's nothing more wonderful than knowing God knows me, loves me and actually wants to talk with me like He would a friend, most of us have the impression God is always on the verge of frustration and pretty much angry with us. We believe if He actually did talk with us, He would be harsh, corrective and impatient. That's certainly the way I believed, and most prophetic words I had heard in church up until that point only served to reinforce my belief.

When I was in my 20s, I was involved in a church whose senior pastor had a prophetic gift. He would speak a prophetic word over every person joining the church as he welcomed them into membership. Although his prophetic words were never harsh or personally embarrassing to anyone, I just *knew* I'd be the first to experience harsh correction or personal embarrassment in front of the whole congregation. As a result, I waited several years to join the church.

Finally, the day came when I decided I did want to become a member of the church, but I knew that meant I would receive a prophetic word from my pastor. As I wrestled with my decision, I finally determined if joining the church meant I was to be corrected and embarrassed, then so be it. On the day I was going to become a member, I was anxious and nervous about what would happen. I was one of about 15 people who were joining the church that day. My pastor made his way through the line of people and then he came to me. He paused for a moment looking intently into my eyes. His look was penetrating. I knew he was seeing deep into my soul and was about to dredge up all my ugliness for everyone to see. I wasn't living sinfully and my heart was turned to God, but I wasn't sure that would matter. I knew I wasn't good enough, and I felt God was barely tolerating me. I was convinced this event was going to draw His ire because it was focusing His attention on me. So I braced myself for a portion of His wrath.

After what seemed like an eternity, my pastor said, "The Lord is not giving me anything for you," and then he moved on to the next person. There was a mixture of relief and frustration. I waited three years for *this*!? Every one of my fellow new members received a prophetic word that day except for me. They were encouraged, affirmed and loved as our pastor shared words from God's heart to each person ... except me. In fact, no one had ever *not* been given a word in all the years I had attended the church! I was the first!

That afternoon, I received a call from my pastor. He comforted me and told me he hadn't felt any sense of sin or God's displeasure over my life for any reason that might prevent God from speaking to me through a prophetic word. He went on to say he was quite puzzled and really couldn't explain why he wasn't given a word for me that morning ... but deep down inside I knew why.

While my pastor shared his thoughts with me, the Lord began to quietly speak to my heart: *I will never embarrass you. If you don't want Me to speak to you, I won't.*

God was gently correcting a misperception I had of Him as He revealed His loving nature to me. That day, I learned He isn't out to hurt or embarrass me. He deals with His children in a loving and private manner.

When I began to understand God wouldn't embarrass me by outing my sins, something happened in my heart that deepened my relationship with Him. I felt more loved by Him that day than I ever had in my whole life. (It's also just like God to bring a corrective explanation directly and discretely to His children as He did to me that day, oftentimes leaving a puzzled minister trying to understand what happened as he himself was out of the communication loop.)

Over the years, as God has allowed me to minister to people through prophetic words, I have never forgotten this experience. I'm always aware of the fear I felt (and that others may feel) in anticipation of receiving a word from God. All ministry for God should accurately reflect His loving care to the people it impacts. Therefore, as prophetic words are delivered, they must lovingly reflect God's desire to be involved in people's lives.

I've been involved in many prophetic presbyteries—a specific time when leaders who have been identified by the church are given words by a prophetic team. The words confirm God's work as the prophetic team identifies and calls forth God-given gifts in leaders and emerging leaders, and they encourage faithful service to God by confirming the focus of ministry. It is a wonderful and anointed time in God's presence for all to enjoy. (We'll go into much greater detail about prophetic presbytery later in the book.) There is also a time at the end of each service for prophetic ministry to individuals in the congregation as God directs through the Holy Spirit's revelation.

Some years ago, I was at a friend's church in Arkansas for a few days of prophetic presbytery. During one of the ministry times, my attention was drawn to a young couple in their late 20s or early 30s. As I began to silently pray about them, the Lord spoke to me and said: *The answer is yes!*

I thought, "OK. But 'yes' what, Lord?"

And He said: *Yes, it is Me that is directing you. Yes, the time is now. And yes, I will bless you! ... Tell them those words.*

Now understand, I had never seen this couple before, I had no idea what was going on in their lives or if this would mean anything to them. What if they stared back at me with a blank expression creating an awkward moment for both of us?

Ultimately, it didn't really matter. I've learned that to be used by God you must be willing to look foolish, and that is certainly true when it comes to prophetic ministry. You ask for and receive revelation from the Holy Spirit; you believe what you receive is from Him; and then you share that revelation with the people God is focusing on. It cannot be confirmed if you're not willing to share it. They will confirm the word by their reaction. A word from God will have the effect of encouraging, building up and comforting the person it is given to either at the time it's received or as it's processed. This process of God's work involves a response of faith by all parties. We respond to *God's* work by receiving the words, and we gain an understanding and application of the words through a response of faith as we process the words with a trusted spiritual leader.

You might wonder, "Could this impression be something from my flesh? Could it be Satan giving me a false word? Is it possible that it's not from God at all?" The answer is yes. If the Holy Spirit is not leading, it can be from our flesh. The key to receiving anything from God is to be surrendered completely to Him and seeking Him as the source of our revelation. Remember this: **the counterfeit of anything never diminishes the real.** Revelation from God and prophetic ministry *is* real.

In Matthew 7, Jesus said:

> *"Ask, and it will be given to you; seek, and you will find; knock, and it will be opened to you. For everyone who asks receives, and he who seeks finds, and to him who knocks it will be opened. Or what man is there among you who, when his son asks for a loaf, will give him a stone? "Or if he asks for a fish, he will not give him a snake, will he? If you then, being evil, know how to give good gifts to your children, how much more will your Father who is in heaven give what is good to those who ask Him!"*
>
> **Matthew 7:7–11, NASB**

Based on Jesus' own words, we can be confident that because we're seeking God and our lives are surrendered to Him the impression we receive won't come from our flesh or Satan, but from God. It is He who is giving us a good thing—an impression to express His love, instill hope in the midst of a troubling situation or provide a word of affirmation and encouragement to someone He cares deeply about. Jesus' promise is clear—our heavenly Father will not allow us to be given a counterfeit or be tricked when we're asking Him to give us something good. Believing this to be absolutely true gives us confidence and supplies us with the boldness to step out in faith to seek and give what we believe is a word from God.

So going back to the couple I received the word for. I stepped off the stage and moved down the aisle toward them. When I reached their seats, I asked them to stand and tell me their names. Then I went ahead and gave the word the Lord had given me. I told them I felt the Lord had spoken to me and asked me to tell them: "The answer is yes! Yes, it is Me who is directing you. Yes, the time is now. And, yes, I will bless you!" As I was speaking those words, the man leaned forward in tears, clutching tightly to the back of the seat in front of him as his wife clung to his arm. People around them responded with affirming support. I had no idea what all this signified, but it seemed to mean something to them as well as others who knew them, and it visibly moved them with emotion. So in response, I asked them, "Do you know what this means?" And they nodded in affirmation.

EVERYONE NEEDS A WORD FROM GOD

As I returned to the stage, the pastor told everyone this couple had been praying about selling their possessions, joining a mission organization and relocating their family to another country to serve as missionaries overseas. That very week, they had sent a letter to the elders of the church asking them to pray about this major decision they were considering. They wanted God's unmistakable confirmation. Needless to say, they got it. They were encouraged, comforted and amazed that God spoke so clearly to confirm His direction for their lives.

And wow ... so was I!! I am still amazed every time God speaks so lovingly and clearly into people's lives.

Although this kind of prophetic ministry usually happens in church during a time set aside in a worship service, I believe God wants prophetic words to be given so naturally even those who don't have a basis for understanding what's happening can receive it and experience God's loving care.

The reality is that people inside the church and outside the church need a loving encounter with God. Imagine if we were to give someone a life-giving word from God in the checkout line at Walmart or at the grocery store or at the gym. Imagine if we were to give our children or a close family member a word like this from the heart of God for whatever situation they might be facing ... a word that wasn't given to them in a religious way but that expressed God's love or brought hope to a troubling situation or even provided direction, affirmation and encouragement from God's heart to theirs.

YOU CAN BE GOD'S DELIVERY AGENT OF A MESSAGE OF ENCOURAGEMENT AND LOVE TO SOMEONE HE CARES FOR DEEPLY.

Everyone needs a word from God! They need to know He cares for them and is aware of the needs and situations in their lives.

My friend, Clark Whitten, experienced this firsthand while he was on a flight en route to participate in a prophetic presbytery at a church. As he was placing his carry-on bag in the overhead bin, he made eye contact with the person who would be sitting next to him on the flight. He had never met the man before and knew nothing about him personally.

As he sat down, Clark asked the man, "So, how is Lucy?" Quite shocked by the question, the man responded, "Do I know you?" Clark said, "No, I don't think we've ever met." The man then asked him again, "How do you know me?" Clark kindly told his flight mate, "I don't know you, and I don't think we've ever met." Clark went on to ask his new acquaintance again, "Do you know Lucy? Who is she, and how is she doing?" Still shocked and a little confused, the man said, "Lucy is my wife, and she's not doing well. She has just been diagnosed with cancer; she has a form of leukemia." Still trying to process what was happening, he again asked Clark, "So, you don't know me *and* you don't know Lucy?"

For the remainder of the flight, Clark was able to share words of hope and encouragement to help this man whom he had never met deal with the devastating news his wife had been given. He was able to share with him the good news of Jesus and God's eternal love. There was no doubt this man and his wife needed a word of hope, encouragement and comfort!

In reality, we *all* need a word from God. Your situation may not be as devastating as Lucy's and her husband's, but it's still critical to you. Do you need a word to give wisdom to a situation or to confirm a direction related to a matter? Do you need a word to reassure you of God's love and action in a circumstance impacting your life? If so, ask Him for a direct word. *His word is life.*

You can be God's delivery agent of a message of encouragement and love to someone He cares for deeply. As you allow God to use you in this way to minister His love to people, my prayer is you'll be challenged and encouraged to step out in faith. And as you do, the Holy Spirit will fill you and use you as His "ministry agent" to help people. When the Apostle Paul was talking to the men of Athens, he said, "Yet He is actually not far from each one of us, for 'in Him we live and move and have our being'" (Acts 17:27–28, ESV). He also wrote: "Now there are varieties of gifts, but the same Spirit. And there are varieties of ministries, and the same Lord. There are varieties of effects, but the same God who works all things in all persons. But to each one is given the manifestation of the Spirit for the common good" (1 Corinthians 12:4–7, NASB). The Holy Spirit is the one who bestows gifts, and His role is to represent Jesus on earth and in our lives.

Also, it's my prayer you'll realize prophetic ministry can be "weird free" when done in an orderly and life-giving manner. The Bible is the *foundation* for all of God's revelation to us. No word or revelation from God will ever be inconsistent with the principles and precepts of the Bible. There are many daily life decisions that aren't specifically addressed in the Bible—where to live, what car to buy, the answer to a family or business dilemma—all these life situations and many others require God's wisdom and direction.

Finally, my hope is you'll gain the perspective that while the prophetic is most often practiced and developed within the context of a church and its ministries, it can also be practiced within the daily context of our lives to encourage, help and comfort people *wherever* we meet them.

2

FOUR SPHERES
OF PROPHECY
Wayne Drain

―――――――

There are different kinds of gifts,
but the same Spirit.

1 Corinthians 12:4 (NIV)

In the 1940s, well-known evangelist Smith Wigglesworth prophesied that around the turn of the century (2000), there would be *a spiritual revival in which the Word and the Spirit would flow together in a fresh and powerful way.* This is an exciting season for the Church across the world. There's an increased hunger and honor for the Word of God in Pentecostal and Charismatic churches. At the same time, we're also seeing a new openness by many in mainline evangelical churches towards the gifts of the Spirit mentioned in 1 Corinthians 12 and Romans 12. This combining of the Word and the Spirit is especially evident in Africa, Central America and South America where the fastest growing churches are those who identify themselves as Charismatic or Pentecostal.

More and more congregations are becoming receptive to the revelation gifts, such as words of knowledge and words of wisdom. There particularly seems to be a growing interest in the area of prophecy. However, there are differing ideas on what prophecy is and how it functions. Many do not believe the gifts of the Spirit (including prophecy) are in operation today. Others believe prophecy is primarily connected to eschatology—the study of the last days or end times.

GENUINE PROPHECY WILL ALWAYS DIRECT PEOPLE TO JESUS, RATHER THAN TO THE PERSON GIVING THE PROPHECY.

As interesting as eschatology is, the focus of this chapter is on understanding the biblical functions of the different spheres of prophecy. I believe there are four distinct spheres of prophecy.

SPHERE #1 ⇥ THE PROPHECY OF SCRIPTURE

This is the first and foremost sphere of prophecy. All biblical revelation prophesied through the Old and New Testament prophets fall into this sphere. We draw all of our scriptural principles concerning prophecy from this sphere. They are our *primary* source for carefully examining words of prophecy given today. The Apostle Peter writes: "Above all, you must understand that no prophecy of Scripture came about by the prophet's own interpretation. For prophecy never had its origin in the human will, but prophets, though human, spoke from God as they were carried along by the Holy Spirit" (2 Peter 1:20–21, NIV). Frank Damazio writes: "The prophecy of Scripture speaks of the declaratory and revelatory elements of the Word of God as the *highest* revelation of God to man."[1] What this means is the logos—the written Word of God—is the highest and purest form of communication from God. But the Apostle Paul also tells us in 1 Corinthians 14 we should desire all the spiritual gifts, *especially the gift of prophecy*. We need both God's written Word and the prophetic word to grow in balance. That's why I believe a prophetic word given must never contradict the principles found in Scripture.

It is God's desire that a prophetic word should be given *as the Holy Spirit leads.* Some are so concerned they might make a mistake that they hold back in fear. Others stride forward through the fog without a thought about the wisdom or timeliness of the words they proclaim. We all need to learn to walk in wisdom and faith. These qualities are not mutually exclusive; they are a team.

SPHERE #2 → A SPIRIT OF PROPHECY

The spirit of prophecy is the anointing of the Holy Spirit that enables men or women who do not have the gift of prophecy or move in the office of the prophet to speak forth under the inspiration of God. Time and time again, it's been my experience that people who may not have a highly visible gift in the area of prophecy can prophesy when an anointing for prophetic ministry is present. That's why I often ask children from our church to pray over me when I have a need or simply need to hear from God. Many times, I feel a small hand gently touch my shoulder and a little voice will speak God's word over my life. I believe, and have seen, when a Spirit of prophecy is present, *everyone* can prophesy—even little children.

In 1 Samuel 10:9-11, we see King Saul prophesied when he was with Samuel's prophetic band. Paul tells us in 1 Corinthians 14:31 that "all can prophesy" when a prophetic anointing is present. However, this can be misunderstood and misapplied, especially when spiritually immature believers have a flippant attitude towards the prophetic. It's equally concerning when individuals use a prophetic gift to draw attention to themselves while seeking fame and fortune.

Through the years, I've noticed genuine prophecy will *always* direct people to Jesus, rather than to the person giving the prophecy. The book of Revelation tells us when John was tempted to fall down and worship an angel, the angel was quick to point him to Jesus as the only one worthy of worship:

At this I fell at his feet to worship him. But he said to me, "Don't do that! I am a fellow servant with you and with your brothers and sisters who hold to the testimony of Jesus. Worship God! For it is the Spirit of prophecy who bears testimony to Jesus."

Revelation 19:10

SPHERE #3 → THE GIFT OF PROPHECY

The gift of prophecy is just that ... a gift. 1 Corinthians 12:4–10 tells us, "There are different gifts, but the same Spirit distributes them ... To one there is given through the Spirit a message of wisdom, to another a message of knowledge by means of the same Spirit ... to another miraculous powers, to another prophecy, to another distinguishing between spirits, to another speaking in different kinds of tongues, and to still another the interpretation of tongues." Prophecy is a gift determined and given by the Holy Spirit. A general rule of thumb is people who have been given a gift of prophecy tend to give words of prophecy with more regularity. And over time, those who are in community with them usually end up recognizing there is a consistency, frequency and accuracy in the number of prophetic words coming from those who have that gift.

People often ask me, "But why do we need prophecy when we have the Scriptures?" While it's true prophecy can never take the place of the Scriptures, the Apostle Paul clearly gives at least three reasons for prophecy in 1 Corinthians: "Follow the way of love and eagerly desire gifts of the Spirit, especially prophecy ... the one who prophesies speaks to people for their strengthening, encouragement and comfort" (1 Corinthians 14:1–3). The gift of prophecy is given to certain believers to bring the word of the Lord to the congregation from the Holy Spirit in order to *strengthen, encourage* and *comfort* God's people.

SPHERE #4 → THE OFFICE OF PROPHET

The final sphere of prophecy is the office of prophet. In the New Testament church in Antioch, we see a man by the name of Agabus was considered to be a prophet because of his *revelation* and *predictions* (Acts 21:10). I believe the realm of foretelling and the confirmation of ministries in the presbytery with the laying on of hands should be done primarily by those who have the mantle of the office of prophet. There are two primary descriptions of the function of this ministry given in the book of Ephesians:

Consequently, you are no longer foreigners and strangers, but fellow citizens with God's people and also members of his household, built on the foundation of the apostles and prophets, with Christ Jesus himself as the chief cornerstone.

Ephesians 2:19–20

It was he [Christ] who gave some to be apostles, some to be prophets, some to be evangelists, and some to be pastors and teachers, to prepare [equip] God's people for [their] works of service, so that the body of Christ may be built up.

Ephesians 4:11–12

A prophet works alongside an apostle to lay foundations in the local church. The office of prophet is one of the grace gifts mentioned in Ephesians, along with the apostle, evangelist, pastor and teacher to equip and train God's people in their work of service. Real prophets don't call attention to themselves; their joy is to equip others to move in the prophetic (if that's their area of service). I get concerned when young ministers refer to themselves as prophets or apostles in an immature way. I'm more comfortable when young men and women refer to themselves as those who move in a prophetic or apostolic anointing. It's always best to let others confirm those designations rather than to declare them over ourselves, because it squelches the Devil's plans to lead us into pride. It's

> **WHEN PROPHETIC MINISTRY IS FUNCTIONING BIBLICALLY AND ACCURATELY, THE CHURCH IS ENCOURAGED TODAY JUST LIKE IT WAS IN THE BOOK OF ACTS.**

also important to note the flip side of that coin is false humility. Don't ever apologize for something the Lord has done in your life. As for me, I want to boldly come before the throne of God so I can walk humbly before Him as I minister to people.

Let me briefly summarize the main points of what we've covered so far:

1. First and foremost, all genuine prophecies must line up with and never contradict the Word of God (2 Peter 1:20–21; 1 Corinthians 4:37).

2. When the Spirit of prophecy is present, all can prophesy (1 Corinthians 14:31).

3. Although we can desire spiritual gifts, it's the *Holy Spirit* who gives gifts as He determines (1 Corinthians 12:11).

4. Not all who prophesy are prophets. The Bible clearly states only certain people are called to be prophets by the Lord and function in that ministry office (Ephesians 4:11–13).

5. Some prophecy has to do with foretelling, revelation and prediction.

6. Let those who prophesy do so with boldness, even as they walk in humility.

Although prophecy can include foretelling, revelations and predictions, it's much broader and deeper than these alone. We live in a time where many are overcome by great discouragement. A dismal economy, wars, hunger, divorce, addictions and the breakdown of morals in society can take their toll on our emotional and spiritual perspective. Our families and churches are being weakened with division and disillusionment. As Frank

Damazio says, "People need the three things that serve as hall-marks for all four spheres of prophecy: strengthening, encouragement and comfort."[2] When prophetic ministry is functioning biblically and accurately, the church is encouraged today just like it was in the book of Acts. For example, during a prophetic presbytery a few years ago, Pastor Brady Boyd prophesied my church would soon enter into a season of great rearrangement and realignment. That word clearly came to pass in the following months, and we were encouraged by the fact that everything that took place was a confirmation of God's word to us.

Acts 13:1–3 provides us with a New Testament example of prophetic presbytery involving the confirmation of a calling and the laying on of hands for leaders like Paul and Barnabas. In our church, we've seen a similar pattern emerge in our yearly prophetic presbyteries—men and women's callings have been confirmed and believers have found courage to take appropriate steps of faith.

Micah and Cindy are a married couple who attend our church. They had been experiencing a growing conviction God was calling them to be missionaries in Taiwan. They agreed together to pray and ask the Lord to have someone prophesy over them, either to confirm what was in their hearts as His will or to help them know if they were missing it. They needed a clear *yes* or *no*! In one of our presbytery services, they received a prophetic word from Pastor Tom Lane that confirmed their

PROPHETIC INSIGHT ABOUT SPECIFIC QUESTIONS OF WHERE, WHEN AND TO WHOM WE ARE CALLED TO IS OF GREAT VALUE.

desire to go to a foreign country and minister (which Pastor Tom mentioned in the previous chapter). The word came with the clarity they needed from a prophet who had *no knowledge* of the couple's prayers! The word was simple: *"Yes, it is Me that is directing you. Yes, the time is now. And yes, I will bless you!"* The door for them to serve as missionaries opened up soon after the word was given, and they went on to enjoy a fruitful season of ministry in Taiwan.

While Micah and Cindy were in Taiwan working with churches and students, they wrestled with the temptation most missionaries face at times to give in to discouragement. Even though the need for salvation was so great, their sense of progress seemed slow. In those times, they found encouragement in reading the Scriptures and remembering the prophetic words over them. The Word and the Spirit flowed together in unison as they cried out to God in prayer. The Scriptures and the prophetic word served to help them fight the fight of faith, just as Timothy was instructed to do by the Apostle Paul in 1 Timothy 1:18–19.

All believers are called to be missionaries. Our commission in Matthew 28:18–20 clearly establishes our call as believers. Our call may be to Taiwan, Tibet, our local Walmart or the neighbors on our street. That's why prophetic insight about specific questions of where, when and to whom we are called to is of great value. This is another reason why the Enemy of our souls doesn't want us to receive prophetic words. He knows they can help us fight the good fight of service and ministry for God. It truly is a *good* fight, because we know that in the end we win!

A spiritually healthy church will have people of all different levels of maturity at any given time. Some are baby Christians who have just been saved. Others may have been faithful servants in the church for years. Still others may have doctorate degrees in theology. It's the same with prophetic ministry. At any given time, we should see people in our churches developing in three of the four spheres of prophecy. Some are just beginning to understand the Scriptures are God's story written by men who were moved by the Holy Spirit. Others may give a prophecy as the Holy Spirit urges them in a particular moment. Others may be regularly expressing a gift of prophecy as a reflection of the ministry God has appointed them to in the congregation. Then there will be those seasoned saints who have become recognized outside their own fellowship of believers as someone with a prophetic ministry—specifically, the type of equipping prophet referred to in Ephesians 4.

As one who travels a great deal, I can say I am seeing at least the beginning of Smith Wigglesworth's prophetic proclamation coming to fruition. For years, it seemed to me most congregations to which I was invited were either primarily focused on understanding the Scriptures or they were focused on the exercise of spiritual gifts. I rarely entered a church that seemed to strike a good balance between the two. More recently, however, I am beginning to see the Word and Spirit flowing together in a more organic expression. Gifts of the Spirit, such as prophecy, are being partnered with the preaching of the Word to equip the saints for their works of service. Preaching and prophesying in the same congregation have been, for the most part, rare, if not completely non-existent with rare exceptions. But something is changing. Combining the Word and the Spirit is becoming a normal part of church life in many congregations. It is truly a marriage made in heaven. We often describe our church as an "evangelical (Bible-based), charismatic" church, and I predict we will see many others operate similarly in the days ahead.

The waters of church life may get a little choppy at times, just like it is when two rivers converge. But as we move downstream with unity and balance, I believe we will see smoother waters that allow the work of God to be released in a fresh and powerful way.

3

WEIGHING
PERSONAL PROPHECY

Wayne Drain

*Two or three prophets should speak, and the others
should weigh carefully what is said.*

1 Corinthians 14:29 (NIV)

My church was birthed during the Jesus Movement of the early 1970s. We were comprised mostly of college and high school students. Established as an elder at 20 years old, I was one of the older members of our group! We were passionate about Jesus and saw many wonderful miracles of salvation and healing in those heady days. Worship, the Baptism in the Holy Spirit and sharing the good news of Jesus were our primary areas of emphasis. Although we had great zeal, we didn't have much wisdom. There were few Bible scholars among us, if any. Needless to say, we had a steep learning curve to negotiate as we aggressively served God and loved people. But God was good and poured out His grace and mercy on us in abundance.

I remember one of my first challenges as an elder and pastor over this group was to figure out what to do with a personal prophecy given in one of our meetings. In that meeting, a beautiful young girl decided to prophesy over herself. She stood up, put her hand on her head and said something like this: "Be encouraged, daughter of the Lord! For the one I have chosen to be your husband is near you ... even now! He is wear-

MISTAKES CAN BE MADE IN THE NAME OF PROPHECY, ESPECIALLY WHEN WE LET OUR DESIRES OR EMOTIONS BECOME THE MOTIVATING FACTOR.

ing a red-checked shirt and has long sideburns. He has not listened to Me, as you have, My daughter. But soon, he will receive My word and ask for your hand in marriage." She sat back down, wearing a particularly blissful expression on her face. I noticed a young man sitting next to her, wearing a red-checked shirt and sporting long sideburns. He was sweating bullets with a fearful look on his face. I didn't know a lot about prophecy at the time other than it was something they did in the book of Acts, which we had just been reading. But in my "knower," I knew this was most likely more *"knowing* in part" than *"prophesying* in part!"

I waited until the meeting was over, and then asked if I could talk to them privately. I remember saying, "Now this *could* be the word of God, but I suspect it was the word of Julie [not her real name]." I told the young man I didn't feel he necessarily had to obey that word since it might not be completely pure. I suggested he seek the Lord and counsel from others he trusted and make sure he examined that word carefully. The young girl looked a little disappointed. The young man looked very relieved! The lesson I learned that day is mistakes can be made in the name of prophecy, especially when we let our desires or emotions become the motivating factor.

In those days, we heard several budding young prophets trying to spread their wings with words like: "Thus saith the Lord:

Yea, Yea, Yea!" One guy actually said: "Thus saith the Lord ... I forgetteth thy name!" It was pretty easy to discern that while this particular word may have been coming from a sincere servant, it wasn't from God. I was pretty sure an all-knowing God wouldn't forget a name! However, we also heard some words of knowledge and words of prophecy I knew were absolutely accurate from people who I knew didn't have any insider information. Therefore, I felt like I needed to be careful not to throw the baby out with the bath water. But how was I to handle judging prophecy? What was I to do with prophetic words that weren't as clearly discernible.

As the leader, I had to judge something I didn't know much about. I quickly learned there's a potential danger in personal prophecy gone goofy if it goes unchecked by wise and discerning leaders. But through the years, I've also learned there's an equal danger when the church reacts to extremes that have been poorly led and mismanaged by rejecting or discouraging personal prophecy altogether.

I decided to grab my Bible concordance and read any passage of scripture I could find dealing with judging or weighing prophecy. What I discovered is Paul said simply: "Prophecy should be judged." In other words, we *are* to check the prophetic words out. But how was I to do that? As I dug a little deeper, I discovered some principles in 1 Thessalonians 5:19–22 (NIV) that have helped me develop some guidelines for examining prophecies: "Do not put out the Spirit's fire; do not treat prophecies with contempt. Test everything. Hold onto the good. Avoid every kind of evil." The Apostle Paul is basically saying here that if we are to judge prophecy in a way that embraces the good and brings redemptive correction wherever the mark has been missed, we need to be open without being naïve and we need to discern without being judgmental. Since then, I have always tried to look for and bring forth the precious, while identifying and letting the worthless go.

I don't want to be overly simplistic in regards to what sometimes can be very complicated situations that come up about giving and receiving prophetic words. However, I feel it's important to share what I have learned and incorporated. Here are four guidelines for weighing personal prophecy that I've used for a long time.

GUIDELINE #1

1 Corinthians 12:11 tells us prophecy is given as the Spirit determines—as He wills. God's Word encourages us to desire spiritual gifts, especially the gift of prophecy (1 Corinthians 14:1), but we don't get to choose which gift we're given. The gifts of the Spirit don't come from a human spirit; they come from the Holy Spirit. So a person can't carry or operate them in his or her own will. These gifts come *as the Holy Spirit wills.*

I have two daughters and a son who are all married now. I once prophesied over a young man who was dating one of my daughters. It wasn't really my plan to give a prophetic word to a guy who was dating one of my daughters. As a dad, I saw it as my job to instill fear in them, not encouragement! I can honestly say it wasn't something I had willed myself to do—quite the opposite, in fact. However, I felt prompted by the Holy Spirit to give the word, and so I did. And in spite of my lack of desire in giving this young man a word from the Lord, I was extremely encouraged when he later told me he felt the Lord's presence in it all. (Full disclosure: this young man is now my son-in-law.)

It's important to understand there are people who are gifted to read other people and they often exploit that gift to get into others' pocketbooks through manipulation. Their gift is a counterfeit of the genuine gift given by the Holy Spirit. An example of this counterfeit expression would be those who engage in fortune telling or psychic phenomena. And just like those who are trained to spot counterfeit money by studying the real thing, we must likewise *train ourselves* to spot genuine prophecy by studying the real thing.

Here are some earmarks of genuine prophecy:

- Genuine prophecy is given for *confirming* and *encouraging*.

- Genuine prophecy will *build up, stir up* and *cheer up.* 1 Corinthians 14:3 tells us: "But the one who prophesies speaks to people for their strengthening, encouraging and comfort."

- Genuine prophecy will never contradict the principles of Scripture. 2 Timothy 3:16 tells us: "All Scripture is God-breathed and is useful for teaching, rebuking, correcting and training in righteousness."

When people give a personal prophecy that isn't in line with God's Word, we should beware. And if it is given in a public meeting, it should be corrected. An example of this would be a prophecy about the exact date Jesus will return, when Jesus Himself clearly said: "But about that day or hour *no one knows*, not even the angels in heaven, nor the Son, but only the Father" (Matthew 24:36; emphasis added). The Holy Spirit will *never* prompt someone to speak a prophetic word that is contrary to Scripture.

Several years ago, a man came and thanked me for teaching him how to hear the voice of the Lord for himself. He went on to say he had disobeyed the Lord, but now he heard Him clearly and was making some changes in order to obey what he had heard. The man said he felt the Lord tell him he had married the wrong woman and the one whom the Lord had really intended him to marry was his secretary. The man told me he was about to start divorce proceedings! When he finished his story and began to thank me again, I interrupted him. I told him there was no doubt he had heard a voice, but it wasn't the voice of the Lord. When he asked me why, I said, "Because a prophetic word will *never* contradict the principles of Scripture." I told him that while there may be biblical reasons for divorcing, his reason definitely did not fit in that category! I encouraged him to go home to his wife, ask for her forgiveness and then seek counseling. Unfortunately, he decided I was the one who wasn't hearing from God and their marriage fell apart. Let me say this as clearly as I can: *We must not allow personal prophecy to usurp the place of Scripture, prayer, godly counsel or the leading of the Holy Spirit in our lives.*

GUIDELINE #2

Weighing prophecy comes from an understanding that prophecy is given to glorify Jesus. Revelation 19:10 says: "For the essence of prophecy is to give a clear witness for Jesus." This also coincides with Jesus' statement that the Holy Spirit would arrive and "glorify Me" (John 16:14). Prophecy should never become too human-centered. By that, I mean prophecy shouldn't ever glorify or benefit an individual more than it does Jesus. An example of this would be using prophecy to enhance the status of someone or to manipulate people to give money or accept certain teachings. The Holy Spirit comes to lift up Jesus, and true prophecy will always bring Him glory.

GUIDELINE #3

Seek counsel from trusted, more mature friends, mentors and those in spiritual authority. Proverbs 13:10 tells us wisdom and safety are found in wise counsel. Ask someone you trust who has spiritual discernment to help you weigh what has been prophesied. Talk about it, pray about it and think about it in a way that allows you a processing and open application of the prophetic word.

GUIDELINE #4

I know this may seem too subjective to some, but the final guideline I use is to listen to my "knower"—the Holy Spirit resident in me. I often tell people, "You'll know in your knower." I believe the Holy Spirit bears witness within us to help us discern when something is right or wrong ... even before we have foolproof evidence. Paul wrote about this in Romans 8:16: "The Spirit Himself bears witness with our spirit." And David was speaking along those same lines when he talked about "deep calling to deep" (Psalm 42:7). There have probably been times in your life when something that was said or done intuitively felt right in your spirit or somehow felt off. If you'll listen to the Holy Spirit within your spirit, you'll grow more spiritually attuned.

The real test of the accuracy of a prophecy is to see if the prophecy comes to pass. There are some if/then words that come from God: "If you'll do this, then I'll do that." But when a word comes with specifics such as dates, names and certain concrete things that are to happen, either it happens or it doesn't. While there is grace for mistakes, public mistakes need to be publicly acknowledged. When we do this, it gives credibility to all genuine prophecy.

Due to false teachings they've received or the potential confusion that can sometimes accompany prophecy, I've seen many church leaders choose to avoid dealing with the prophetic altogether by banning its practice in their churches. However, I've discovered over the years people are hungry for genuine prophetic gifts. One word from God regarding situations in our lives changes everything. There have been times when I've seen unbelievers who were totally unaware of prophecy come to the Lord in salvation directly due to a prophetic word. In 1 Corinthians 14:24–25, Paul describes a service where genuine prophetic expression was allowed: "But if all of you are prophesying, and unbelievers or people who don't understand these things come into your meeting, they will be convicted of sin and judged by what you say. As they listen, their secret thoughts will be exposed, and they will fall to their knees and worship God, declaring, 'God is truly here among you.'"

In his book, *2000 Years of Charismatic Christianity*, Eddie Hyatt writes: "For prophecy to be used for its greatest benefit, we must avoid the extremes of a too-controlled or an uncontrolled prophetic ministry. A too-controlled approach will quench the gift altogether, while the uncontrolled approach will inevitably lead to misuse, abuse and disaster."[1] As a pastor and worship leader, I can tell you this balance isn't always easy to achieve.

Pastor John Wimber once said, "Sometimes God offends our mind to reveal our heart."[2] At times, we can immediately see what a prophetic word means in our lives, and it's easy to trust God because we understand. But sometimes, when it's hard to understand what a prophetic word means, it's good to follow the example of Mary, the mother of Jesus, when Gabriel announced God's word to her—we do what she did and just hold the word in our hearts and choose to trust God to either confirm the word or let it be revealed as inaccurate.

Do not avoid judging prophecies when they are given publicly, but judge without being judgmental. Use the guidelines we've laid out in this chapter to protect God's expression in your community. When you bear witness or agree with a word, you can affirm and encourage the one who gave it. But if a word is given that you aren't sure of, the most loving thing you can do is to examine, weigh and judge the word carefully while kindly and openly communicating with the person giving the word and whoever is receiving the word. This is required if you are a pastor, elder or leader, but it is also true if you're a friend or a mentor to the person who gave the word. If you feel you must disagree or question a prophecy, you should do so as redemptively as possible, with humility. You always want to handle yourself in a way that protects the dignity of others. It might help to remember personal mistakes you've made in the past as you lead in this area of ministry, because it will give you a gentle compassion as you guide and correct those ministering in the prophetic. Thank God for His amazing grace and for speaking to us through His Holy Spirit today!

The Purpose of New Testament Prophetic Ministry

4

TO EQUIP FOR SERVICE AND MINISTRY

Tom Lane

———

Our relationship with God comes with eternal purpose and current responsibilities. Every servant of God is responsible for finding their useful place of ministry for God and His kingdom. Paul spoke of this process in his letter to the church in Ephesus:

And He Himself gave some to be apostles, some prophets, some evangelists, and some pastors and teachers, for the equipping of the saints for the work of ministry, for the edifying of the body of Christ, till we all come to the unity of the faith and of the knowledge of the Son of God, to a perfect man, to the measure of the stature of the fullness of Christ; that we

should no longer be children, tossed to and fro and carried
about with every wind of doctrine, by the trickery of men, in
the cunning craftiness of deceitful plotting.

Ephesians 4:11–14, NKJV

As a new believer back in the 1970s and 1980s, my experience with the church and ministries that were designed to strengthen and mature the believer didn't seem to match what I saw in the New Testament as a model for equipping and maturing the church. This was *especially* true as it related to prophetic ministry. Most of the people recognized for having a prophetic gift weren't pastors or elders. In fact, many didn't even have any kind of leadership role in a specific church. They usually had an itinerant ministry independent of any specific local church. They traveled and ministered in many churches they weren't a part of and didn't have leadership involvement in any single local church.

When these prophets came to minister, the church as a whole was usually on edge. After all, they were supposed to be God's representatives relaying a message directly from Him. The content of their message was more often than not corrective, and their ministry was to expose sin and serve as God's voice to call His wayward children back into relationship with Him. Personally, I felt the ministry of the prophetic was like a scheduled spanking from God ... it wasn't pleasant, but it seemed necessary. Whenever these prophets left, I didn't feel built up or equipped. My thought was always: "Wow, I'm glad we got that over!" No one had ever taught me the difference between the prophetic ministry modeled in the Old Testament and the new model of prophetic ministry in the New Testament.

In the first chapter of Acts, the disciples gathered in the Upper Room as they awaited the promised coming of the Holy Spirit. We know this event as Pentecost, but it was so much more than just a group of believers having an encounter with God in an upper room with tongues of fire on their head and unknown languages being spoken. The Holy Spirit was specifically sent by Jesus after His resurrection to bring God's indwelling presence to each believer. It was to *every* believer's advantage for the Holy Spirit to come into their life and reside in their hearts in order to bring the presence of God personally to them. In addition, it was through the Holy Spirit's work He would bestow grace gifts on them and work through them to impact the world. This resident presence of the Holy Spirit in each believer's life changed the function of the prophetic office from what it was in the Old Testament to a different purpose in the New Testament. In the Old Testament, God's presence did not dwell with men but in His temple. God related to men through His chosen representatives as they had asked Him to at Mount Sinai (Exodus 20:18–21).

IT TAKES REVELATION, FAITH, INSIGHT AND LEADING FROM THE HOLY SPIRIT TO KNOW THE EXACT WORDS NEEDED IN A SPECIFIC MOMENT OF TIME TO CONFIRM WHAT GOD IS DOING OR SAYING.

In the New Testament, the Holy Spirit brought God's presence to every believer—leading them into all truth, guiding them in the way they should go and convicting them of sin, righteousness and judgment. There was no longer a need for a prophet to fulfill those particular functions.

Generally speaking, the Old Testament prophets tended to be separate from the general population and daily life of the nation. They remained apart so they could stay uncompromised as they spoke declarations of God's frustration and displeasure to the nation and to its governing leaders as well as exposing their sins and directing them to repent. The Bible clearly records over and over that as a result, they were resisted, rejected and killed for their efforts. In contrast, the New Testament prophets were part of the community of believers. And as a part of that community, they participated in the life and leadership of the church. The individual expression of the prophetic became a part of the ministry of the church as each person exercised their gifts in service to God and each other.

In his first letter to the Corinthians, the Apostle Paul talked about the Holy Spirit's gifts and the expression of those gifts within the community of believers. In chapter 14, he directed believers to strongly and earnestly desire all the gifts of the Spirit, but to especially desire the gift of prophecy. His reason for this specific encouragement was his awareness of what prophetic ministry accomplishes—it builds up, gives exhortation and brings comfort to believers and the church as a whole. It takes revelation, faith, insight and leading from the Holy Spirit to know the exact words needed in a specific moment of time to confirm what God is doing or saying. It also takes this same faith and inspiration to speak words that bring clarity to a specific direction and may even correct some confusion relating to a matter taking place in a specific individual's life or the general church body.

The book of Acts (also known as the Acts of the Apostles) gives us a picture of the work of the prophets in the church. No longer did prophets stay outside the camp speaking into the life of the community of believers. Now they were a part of the community, working in tandem with those operating in other gifts to strengthen and encourage the church together (Acts 11:27; Acts 13:1; Acts 15:32; Acts 21:10; 1 Corinthians 14:31). They were members of a *team* who came together with one purpose—to equip the saints for the work of ministry so everyone might mature and grow in their ability to serve God and people (Ephesians 4:11). Paul likened this work of the church to that of the human body— each member reflects a given part and all parts are necessary for the body to function properly (1 Corinthians 12:14).

We see the prophetic gift at work in the church and the lives of the believers in some very specific ways.

1. **Prophetic Ministry Identifies Gifts and Callings**
   The Bible clearly declares God has given each person gifts that are to be used in service for Him. 1 Timothy 4:14–16 (NKJV) instructs us by saying:

Do not neglect the gift that is in you, which was given to you by prophecy with the laying on of the hands of the eldership. Meditate on these things; give yourself entirely to them, that your progress may be evident to all. Take heed to yourself and to the doctrine. Continue in them, for in doing this you will save both yourself and those who hear you.

The discovery and deployment of our God-given gifts is a *lifelong* process. For anyone who's sincere about knowing and doing God's will, it's always encouraging and exciting to have the specific application of those gifts in your life identified and confirmed. When someone other than yourself identifies and substantiates your abilities or place of service, it can bring great confidence and peace.

This is what happened to Timothy when the Apostle Paul wrote to remind him, and it still happens today. I was once on a prophetic team who spoke over a married couple. They were unknown to us, but as we spoke out the impressions the Holy Spirit was giving us, we identified they had a call to ministry with specific gifts of administration. This word was in keeping with what God had already been speaking to them personally, and our prophetic confirmation gave them peace and confidence. Unknown to us, the husband had been talking with the church leadership about leaving his job and stepping into an administrative pastoral role on their team. They were looking for God to confirm his move out of his business career and into this place of vocational ministry. Through prophetic ministry, they received a rock-solid confirmation from heaven!

2. **Prophetic Ministry Clarifies Direction for Life and Ministry**
Our daily lives are filled with danger and peril, and it's often difficult for us to identify with our natural eyes all

that awaits us through every opportunity that comes our way. Will it succeed or fail? Is it God's will or not? Should I take this job? Should I move to this city? Should I accept this ministry assignment? Life is filled with necessary and important questions that must be answered.

We don't often think of these questions in the context of life or death, but that's because we tend to measure them in one dimension—the physical. As important as that is, what about the spiritual dimension? Have you ever done something or committed to something, but once you became involved, you quickly realized it had no life to it? Instead, it was robbing you of life and energy and putting your emotional, spiritual and maybe even physical, life at risk. That's why we so desperately need God's confirmation for the direction and decisions of our lives!

Acts 21:10–14 (NLT) tells us the story of one such incident where a prophetic word helped solidify the Apostle Paul's decision to go to Jerusalem:

> *Several days later a man named Agabus, who also had the gift of prophecy, arrived from Judea. He came over, took Paul's belt, and bound his own feet and hands with it. Then he said, "The Holy Spirit declares, 'So shall the owner of this belt be bound by the Jewish leaders in Jerusalem and turned over to the Gentiles.'" When we heard this, we and the local believers all begged Paul not to go on to Jerusalem. But he said, "Why all this weeping? You are breaking my heart! I am ready not only to be jailed at Jerusalem but even to die for the sake of the Lord Jesus." When it was clear that we couldn't persuade him, we gave up and said, "The Lord's will be done."*

Although I've seen God give clarity and confirmation through prophetic ministry many times, each time it happens I'm filled with wonder and awe at God's loving care for His sons and daughters. While I was ministering at a church, I called out a man sitting toward the back during the service. He didn't look neat or dapper as if he had it all together; instead, he looked cynical and discouraged, a complete mess. I told him God wanted to let him know He hadn't forgotten him. I went on to tell him he had an ability he wasn't using in a way he wanted to or, for that matter, in a way God ever intended for him to use it. I told him, if he was willing, God would make a way for him to get back in service. I asked him if he knew how this applied to his life, and he nodded in affirmation. After the service, he told me he was new to the church; he had only been attending for a few weeks. He was a musician and had been active in the church when he was younger, but he had been away for a while and was just now coming back to the Lord and to the church. That word was a message to him directly from God to let him know he was welcome home and there was a place for him and his musical gifts. He had been playing in clubs and bars and thought there wouldn't be an opportunity for him to use his musical ability in church. I've been back to that church many times, and it's always so awesome to see him actively participating on the worship team and to see him active in the life of the church. God's work is amazing!

3. **Prophetic Ministry Confirms God's Word, Direction and Presence in Circumstances**

   Our lives are to be lived in partnership with God and should involve the passionate pursuit of His plans and purposes. When we live with this perspective, we look for His hand in all the circumstances of our lives. This is the way the disciples lived, and it's still God's plan for us today.

   Once again, there's a great example of this from the life of the Apostle Paul:

The terrible storm raged for many days, blotting out the sun and the stars, until at last all hope was gone. No one had eaten for a long time. Finally, Paul called the crew together and said, "Men, you should have listened to me in the first place and not left Crete. You would have avoided all this damage and loss. But take courage! None of you will lose your lives, even though the ship will go down. For last night an angel of the God to whom I belong and whom I serve stood beside me, and he said, 'Don't be afraid, Paul, for you will surely stand trial before Caesar! What's more, God in his goodness has granted safety to everyone sailing with you.' So take courage! For I believe God. It will be just as he said. But we will be shipwrecked on an island."

Acts 27:20–26, NLT

Several years ago, I was giving words to individuals during a prophetic ministry service. I asked a young Hispanic couple (whom I later learned were very new to the congregation) to stand, and I began to describe a picture I'd seen that I thought applied to their lives. I saw them stopped at a railroad crossing. They were waiting in their car behind the railroad crossing bar, but a train wasn't coming. The impression I had was they were being tempted to go around the crossing bar. I felt led to encourage them to be patient and not go around the crossing bar. I told them God was at work in all of the circumstances surrounding their delay, so be patient and be careful not to act impulsively or carelessly. I asked them if they understood how this word applied to them, and with tears flowing, they nodded yes. After the service, they came to tell me the husband was in the country as an illegal immigrant and had been here for seven years. While he was here, he had gone to college, graduated and married his wife (who was here legally). They had attempted to change his status but weren't having any success. As an illegal immigrant, he was unable to work and lived every day with the fear of being deported. There were some close friends and family members who advised him to just move on and live life—to go around the crossing bar—by looking for a job and expecting not to be caught. They encouraged him to start a family and not worry about being deported. He was hesitant to do that; he needed confirmation of some direction to take in order to get his life unstuck. Through the prophetic word God gave me for that couple, he received confirmation and was able to connect with a lawyer in the congregation who specialized in immigration law. What's more, he was so new to the congregation, the pastor didn't even know him or his situation ... but God did!

5

TO GIVE CLARITY TO GOD'S WORK IN THE CHURCH AND ON EARTH

Tom Lane

———

For through Him we both have access by one Spirit to the Father.
Now, therefore, you are no longer strangers and foreigners,
but fellow citizens with the saints and members of
the household of God, having been built on the foundation
of the apostles and prophets, Jesus Christ Himself
being the chief cornerstone, in whom the whole building,
being fitted together, grows into a holy temple in the Lord,
in whom you also are being built together
for a dwelling place of God in the Spirit.

Ephesians 2:18–22 (NKJV)

Spiritual gifts are given to individuals and expressed within groups for the purpose of building, encouraging and comforting the saints of God. When prophetic ministry is recognized and embraced by the church in a healthy way, its impact on individuals and influence on the work of the church is powerful. I've personally been blessed tremendously to experience its benefit in my own life.

It's hard to describe the delivery of prophetic words or prophetic ministry in one specific way because God uses individuals to speak the word, and I believe He allows the flavor of their personality and individuality to come out as they express the gift. This is one way we, as His servants, partner with God in ministry. According to the Bible, the gifts of the Spirit are distributed by the Holy Spirit for different kinds of service and works. In 1 Corinthians 12:4–6 (NIV), Paul wrote, "There are different kinds of gifts, but the same Spirit distributes them. There are different kinds of service, but the same Lord. There are different kinds of working, but in all of them and in everyone it is the same God at work." Paul was saying there are different kinds of gifts, service and work because God uses individuals to minister, but through it all, God is at work helping people.

God often uses individuals to speak a prophetic word that encourages, challenges and comforts to build others up. Sometimes He uses individuals in this way so a church's leadership recognizes that person as having a ministry in the prophetic. Other times, God simply chooses for an individual to be His agent "for the moment" by delivering His word to build up the church or the individual. Either way, the Holy Spirit uses the gift of the prophetic to build up believers and the church. Although the power and impact of God's work can be experienced in many ways in our lives, He uses the prophetic gift to specifically confirm His work, encourage His children and comfort and bless the church.

The New Testament gives us several examples of times when God's prophetic voice was expressed in the church. The book of Acts relates the following incident:

> *Now in the church that was at Antioch there were certain prophets and teachers: Barnabas, Simeon who was called Niger, Lucius of Cyrene, Manaen who had been brought up with Herod the tetrarch, and Saul.* **As they ministered to the Lord and fasted, the Holy Spirit said, "Now separate to Me Barnabas and Saul for the work to which I have called them."** *Then, having fasted and prayed, and laid hands on them, they sent them away.*
>
> **Acts 13:1–3 (NKJV; emphasis added)**

The work of ministry involves helping people as we lead and govern the church in a way that pleases the Lord. Every time we're faced with a decision on how to move forward with ministry, our desire should be to know the mind of God so we can accomplish His will by doing what *He* wants. However, there *are* times in the process of discovering what God wants us to do in a situation that we arrive at an impasse and don't know what to do next. Those are the times when, despite our countless efforts and discussions, we're unable to determine a clear direction. We struggle to know God's will on a matter and how to specifically move forward. As we seek counsel from godly friends and mentors and as each one gives their perspective, the right decision becomes less clear based on the variety of options being presented. When individuals are passionately presenting their own perspectives (as godly and biblical as they may be), it gets difficult to clearly identify what the Lord's mind is on the matter. Therefore, it's hard to know how to move forward. Each individual feels like they know or have represented God's perspective. As they share their perspective, they're seeking to influence the direction and the outcome of the discussion with godly motivation.

To avoid this confusion, it's easy to neglect the process of seeking counsel on important decisions of direction. It's also difficult to find specific direction from God's Word that might relate to what, when and how to deal with a specific situation in our lives. If we want to follow God and we're looking for His perspective through a variety of perspectives, it can definitely be a struggle to find agreement and come to a place of unity relating to a decision. What we need is a word from God! Ultimately, when the process

GOD OFTEN USES INDIVIDUALS TO SPEAK A PROPHETIC WORD THAT ENCOURAGES, CHALLENGES AND COMFORTS TO BUILD OTHERS UP.

is centered around what God is saying, we can find agreement and come to a place of unity. When we find this unity, we also find peace, which is one of the primary marks of God's wisdom and direction.

Acts 3 tells us there were certain prophets and teachers in the church. These men and women were known in the church and connected in relationship with others in the church. In other words, they were doing life together. I imagine in the course of doing life together they also had different perspectives on issues at times. The passage simply says the Holy Spirit gave them direction as they ministered to the Lord and fasted; it doesn't say exactly *how* He gave them direction. I personally believe this direction came through the individual expression of their gifts. Teachers would tend to see things from a "how" perspective and represent that perspective passionately. On the other hand, those with a prophetic gift would see it from more of a "what" and "why" perspective. At some point in their discussions, clarity was reached as they combined their perspectives to understand the "what," "why" and "how" of the way God wanted them to move forward. And as a result of their unity, they were able to move forward with a clear direction.

> ## THE CONTENT OF THE WORD AND HOW IT'S DELIVERED MUST ALWAYS REPRESENT THE HEART OF GOD.

Although I highly doubt the discussions were mean-spirited or the individuals were stubborn, I'm sure each person was passionately convinced of their perspective and represented it with confidence. In the midst of these discussions—without a "thus saith the Lord" or a religious announcement meant to dominate or control—one of the team with a prophetic gifting would introduce a Holy Spirit-directed perspective that connected the diverse perspectives represented in the conversation. It could even come as an "aha" moment. With simple clarity, the words would identify the heart of the issue, give clarity to the perspectives expressed and open the door for those of different perspectives to come together in unity around what God was speaking about the matter at hand.

The power of this kind of prophetic work is in its relational unity. It didn't force one person's perspective of what God was saying upon the group. Instead, it was a team of leaders sharing their individual perspectives on issues, and a prophetic word summarized God's direction to the group. In the midst of sharing, prophetic insight and clarity was brought forth pointing all involved to what God was desiring in the situation.

The Holy Spirit speaks and gives us revelation of God's will and direction for our lives. And when His Spirit speaks to us, God expects us to respond with obedient faith. A great example of this kind of obedience can be seen in the life of Philip.

> *As for Philip, an angel of the Lord said to him, "Go south down the desert road that runs from Jerusalem to Gaza." So he started out, and he met the treasurer of Ethiopia, a eunuch of great authority under the Kandake, the queen of Ethiopia. The eunuch had gone to Jerusalem to worship, and he was now returning. Seated in his carriage, he was reading aloud from the book of the prophet Isaiah. The Holy Spirit said to Philip, "Go over and walk along beside the carriage." Philip ran over and heard the man reading from the prophet Isaiah. Philip asked, "Do you understand what you are reading?" The man replied, "How can I, unless someone instructs me?" And he urged Philip to come up into the carriage and sit with him.*
>
> **Acts 8:26–32 (NLT)**

The Holy Spirit also gives revelation to individuals in a corporate setting in order to use them in His service as He brings clarity and direction. When revelation is given through a prophetic word, it will either give clarity to a ministry situation, warn an individual of the results of their actions and behaviors or confirm a decision that's been made or is being made. The key is the method and motive of delivery. A prophetic word should be delivered in a positive, encouraging and comforting manner. It shouldn't be given out of harshness, with a critical spirit or in a way that is aggressive and mean-spirited. The content of the word and how it's delivered must always represent the heart of God, or else you can rightly conclude it's not from God.

Once again, the book of Acts is full of great examples showing us how the prophetic should operate within the church.

> *And in these days prophets came from Jerusalem to Antioch. Then one of them, named Agabus, stood up and showed by the Spirit that there was going to be a great famine throughout all the world, which also happened in the days of Claudius Caesar. Then the disciples, each according to his ability, determined to send relief to the brethren dwelling in Judea. This they also did, and sent it to the elders by the hands of Barnabas and Saul.*
>
> Acts 11:27–30 (NKJV)

> *So when they were sent off, they came to Antioch; and when they had gathered the multitude together, they delivered the letter. When they had read it, they rejoiced over its encouragement.* **Now Judas and Silas, themselves being prophets also, exhorted and strengthened the brethren with many words.** *And after they had stayed there for a time, they were sent back with greetings from the brethren to the apostles.*
>
> Acts 15:30–33 (NKJV; emphasis added)

> *And when we had finished our voyage from Tyre, we came to Ptolemais, greeted the brethren, and stayed with them one day. On the next day we who were Paul's companions departed and came to Caesarea, and* **entered the house of Philip the evangelist, who was one of the seven, and stayed with him. Now this man had four virgin daughters who prophesied. And as we stayed many days, a certain prophet named Agabus came down from Judea. When he had come to us, he took Paul's belt, bound his own hands and feet, and said, "Thus says the Holy Spirit, 'So shall the Jews at Jerusalem bind the man who owns this belt, and deliver him into the hands of the Gentiles.'"** *Now when we heard these things, both we and those from that place pleaded with him not to go up to Jerusalem. Then Paul answered, "What do you mean*

by weeping and breaking my heart? For I am ready not only to be bound, but also to die at Jerusalem for the name of the Lord Jesus." So when he would not be persuaded, we ceased, saying, "The will of the Lord be done."

Acts 21:7–14 (NKJV; emphasis added)

Understanding and believing that this pattern of New Testament work is still applicable today, I was praying one afternoon for a service I was going to attend that evening. As I prayed, I had an impression. I saw a man in my mind, and I knew without a doubt he would be in the service that night. The Holy Spirit gave me a picture of a specific situation related to the man. I saw that the man had been injured in a tractor accident some time back ... maybe years before. It was at least long enough that his injuries had long healed. The impression I had was the tractor had rolled, pinning the man's right leg and damaging his knee. As I processed what I was seeing in my spirit, I knew his knee was hurting and the prophetic word I got for the man was that God wanted to reveal himself to the man that night in a special way through revealing the situation and healing his pain. At

IF YOU'RE MINISTERING PROPHETICALLY, YOU CAN'T ASSUME YOUR PROPHETIC INSIGHT IS ALWAYS FULLY ACCURATE OR DELIVERED WITH PERFECT TIMING.

an appropriate time in the service, I stepped forward and told the congregation of the word and asked if there was a man present who fit those circumstances. I waited for someone to respond. The moments that followed felt like hours, but was probably only seconds. After what seemed to be a long time with no response, I apologized for my mistake and turned to sit down.

Let me interrupt my story for a few moments to emphasize an important point of prophetic accountability: When we minister prophetically, we must be willing to humble ourselves if the word we deliver doesn't fit the situation or the person receiving it.

There are many times when we deliver a word to someone who is intimidated by the public exposure, so they act totally unresponsive to the word as it's delivered. Sometimes a person doesn't realize the application of the word for their situation until a friend or loved one makes the application for them. If you're ministering prophetically, you can't assume your prophetic insight is always fully accurate or delivered with perfect timing. You must be willing to acknowledge that even though you have a right heart of obedient service, you can miss what God is doing or saying in a situation. Out of that sense of integrity before God and people, I apologized since there wasn't an application for the word with those present.

The pastor, however, stopped me and encouraged me to try again saying he felt the word was accurate and applied to someone there. So at his request, I faced the congregation and described the circumstances one more time and waited for a response. After what seemed like another eternity, a man in the back of the auditorium stood up, pointed to a man seated a few rows from where I was standing and called him by name. The man from the back of the auditorium told his friend to stand up because he knew the word was directly for him. Slowly the man stood up, and I asked him if he was injured in a tractor accident. He nodded yes. I then asked him if it injured his right leg and knee, and he nodded yes a second time. When I asked him if it was hurting him at that moment, he once again nodded yes. So I prayed for God to take away the pain and heal the man. Right then and there, God healed the man!

It's moments like those when there is *no* denying God knows the intimate details of our lives and is continually at work!

Is it possible you need some clarity from God relating to His direction or work in your life? While it's definitely true God speaks to us through His written Word, it's equally true He makes clear and specific application of His desires in the circumstances of our lives at strategic times through a prophetic word. A prophetic word can bring clarity, direction, encouragement and peace to situations in our marriage or important issues relating to the future. It can also impact directional decisions for our children and give us clarity about God's desire to use us in ministry for Him. When we open our hearts to embrace His prophetic words spoken to us, we embrace Him and His work in our lives.

> *Now you are the body of Christ, and members individually. And God has appointed these in the church: first apostles, second prophets, third teachers, after that miracles, then gifts of healings, helps, administrations, varieties of tongues. Are all apostles? Are all prophets? Are all teachers? Are all workers of miracles? Do all have gifts of healings? Do all speak with tongues? Do all interpret?*
>
> **1 Corinthians 12:27–30 (NKJV)**

> *Do not neglect the gift that is in you, which was given to you by prophecy with the laying on of the hands of the eldership. Meditate on these things; give yourself entirely to them, that your progress may be evident to all.*
>
> **1 Timothy 4:14–15 (NKJV)**

6

TO PARTNER WITH PROCLAIMING THE GOSPEL

Wayne Drain

---

*"But you will receive power when the Holy Spirit
comes on you; and you will be my witnesses in Jerusalem,
and in all Judea and Samaria, and to the ends of the earth."*

Acts 1:8 (NIV)

When we accept that the Holy Spirit and His gifts are operating in people's lives today, it's tempting to focus that powerful ministry inward and make the church a "bless me" club. However, it's not at all what God intended when He sent the Holy Spirit to bring His presence in our lives. I was recently invited to speak at a church just outside London, England. I titled the message I planned to share: "It's Time to Put the 'E' Back in Missions." You're probably thinking, "But wait, there isn't an 'e' in the word 'missions'!" And you're right, but I intentionally chose to title my message that way to highlight the need for "<u>e</u>vangelism"—proclaiming the good news of the gospel of Jesus Christ. I wanted to point out that much of what we do in our missions efforts nowadays, although helpful to many, tends to leave out the central ingredient of sharing the good news of Jesus—the opportunity for someone to pray and receive Jesus as their Savior and Lord. All around the world, believers are feeding and clothing the poor, speaking out against injustices and attempting to heal the broken in the name of Jesus. And that is definitely all wonderful; however, it's my observation

EVANGELISM—OR SHARING ONE'S FAITH— IS SOMETHING MOST CHRISTIANS BELIEVE THEY SHOULD DO, BUT ONLY A SMALL PERCENTAGE ACTUALLY DO.

that too often we get cold feet and miss an opportunity when we don't offer people the chance to receive Christ as their Savior.

My invitation to speak in London came from a pastor who was concerned that even though members of his congregation were great at loving and helping people in practical ways, many were missing the most important point. The church was helping people with very basic areas of need, and no doubt many of those being helped were making the connection to what motivated Christians to serve in this manner. However, this British pastor had come to the conclusion if they weren't at least offering people the opportunity to come to Christ through salvation, they weren't really helping people find any real solution for their situation.

Towards the end of the service, I asked a young African woman to assist me in illustrating how to lead someone to salvation. Because she was sitting near the front, I assumed she was a member of the church. As we went through the exercise, I came to the point of asking her if she would like to come to Christ. That's when something unexpected happened. The young lady began to softly weep. When I inquired if she was alright, she simply said, "I have not received Jesus, but I want to." To my delight, this role-playing for the sake of an illustration had turned into a reality show! With great joy, I prayed with her to receive Jesus in salvation, and the congregation rejoiced with us! Later that day, nine others joined the young lady in receiving Jesus!

After the meeting, I asked the woman why she had chosen to give her life to Christ. She responded by saying, "I was just waiting for someone to ask me." I later found out from the pastor she had been living in an apartment with Christian roommates for the past six months and had been attending church during that time. But no one had ever asked her if she would like to receive Christ. Like that young lady, there are countless people in the "valley of decision" (Joel 3:14) who are just waiting for someone to share the good news of Jesus with them. The events that took place in that service more than confirmed the pastor's concern that his congregation was leaving the "e" out of missions.

Throughout church history, there have been various methods used for winning people to Christ. One such method of evangelism used in the United States is Evangelism Explosion (EE)—a successful program that teaches Christian men and women to share their faith in a compelling way.[1] A qualified EE leader guides people through a period of training, and eventually, teams are sent door to door offering non-believers an opportunity to come to salvation. The idea behind it involves a type of "playing the averages" method: for every ten doors you knock on, one person will be interested in coming to know Christ. I thank God for the thousands of souls who have walked out of the darkness of their sin and into Jesus' marvelous light of salvation through EE. A problem with this method, however, is that it can be quite intimidating for many people to go door to door like this. Many people simply cannot get over their fear of getting it wrong, and as a result, most Christians simply avoid participating in this kind of evangelism.

Evangelism—or sharing one's faith—is something most Christians believe they *should* do, but only a small percentage actually do. Many prefer to leave evangelism to the experts. Unfortunately, this robs so many of the incomparable joy that comes from praying with someone to be born again. As someone who believes every believer should respond to the

Great Commission to go and make disciples of all nations (Matthew 8:18–20), I have spent a considerable amount of thought and prayer to find a solution to help others share their faith.

In 2006, during one of those times of prayer, a picture popped into my mind. I saw two vases; one was filled with marbles and the other was empty. The vase with marbles had black chains. The empty vase had white crosses. Then I saw hands reaching in and moving marbles from the filled jar into the empty jar ... one marble at a time. I knew the idea behind that image was whenever someone comes to salvation, a marble is moved from the vase covered in chains to the vase with white crosses to celebrate someone being born again. It was a visual representation of someone coming out of darkness into God's marvelous light (1 Peter 2:9). As I reflected on what I was seeing, I felt led to recreate it by painting one vase with black chains and another with white crosses. Since sharing that picture with my congregation, it has captured their imagination and hearts. We have seen a steady and continual increase in the number of salvations in our church. In 2010 alone, we saw more salvations than in the previous five years combined! This prophetic picture has inspired our congregation to get personally invested in sharing their faith. And today, it's one of the highlights of our services when people come forward to share a brief testimony about someone who has come to salvation and they move a marble from one vase to the other. It's especially wonderful when the one who actually prayed to receive Christ comes forward to move a marble that represents their move from darkness into light.

I believe there are two basic motivations behind why it's necessary for the church to put the "e" back into missions.

1. A Motivation to Love

The Great Commandment of Matthew 22:36–40 tells us to *love God* and *love our neighbor*. This is what motivates us to feed and clothe the poor, to speak out for those who have no voice and to share the good news of

Jesus to those coming to salvation. Love is the greatest motivator I know for putting the "e" in missions.

2. A Mandate to Share our Faith

Some believers behave as though the Great Commission in Matthew 28:18–20 is actually the "Great Suggestion." I promise you, it was never intended to be a suggestion. It is a mandate from our Lord to His followers. It is a mandate to *"go into all the world and make disciples."* It's as simple as that. We accomplish this by carrying out the same elements of ministry that Jesus referred to in Luke 4:16–21 when he stood up in the synagogue and quoted from the book of Isaiah:

a. Preaching the good news to the poor and binding up the brokenhearted.

b. Proclaiming freedom for the prisoners and recovery of sight for the blind and comforting all who mourn.

c. Releasing the oppressed and proclaiming the year of the Lord.

Most Christians would agree the Great Commandment and Great Commission were given by the Lord Jesus. What we seem to need though is a method that works. We've done everything from knocking on doors to organizing tent revivals and open air concerts. We've painted faces, juggled stuff and put up climbing walls to get people's attention. While none of these efforts are wrong, they're often ineffective.

Over the past few years, we've seen more and more people coming to salvation when we simply cooperate with the leading of the Holy Spirit. Personally, I would rather knock on one door the Holy Spirit has led me to than knock on one hundred doors and hope ten will respond.

So how can we partner, or cooperate, with the Holy Spirit for effective evangelism? I found some answers to this question in the biblical story of Philip the Evangelist. The Bible tells us he was one of seven deacons chosen to serve the elders. These men were "known to be full of the Spirit and wisdom" (Acts 6:3, NIV). And because of their servants' hearts, "the word of God spread, the number of disciples increased rapidly and a large number of priests became obedient to the faith" (Acts 6:7, NIV). Later, in Acts 8, we see that Philip went down to a city in Samaria and proclaimed Christ there. He also performed miraculous signs, cast out evil spirits and many paralytics and cripples were healed. Philip *invested* himself in sharing his faith.

As I read the account of Philip leading the Ethiopian eunuch to Christ in Acts 8:26–40, I began to notice a strong partnership between the gifts of the Holy Spirit and evangelism. The passage shows us that the Holy Spirit directed Philip to head down a specific road going from Jerusalem to Gaza. While on that road, Philip met an Ethiopian official on his way home from worshiping in Jerusalem. The Spirit directed Philip to go to the chariot and stay near it. As he ran alongside the chariot, Philip heard the eunuch reading from the book of Isaiah—the Holy Spirit was already at work in this man's heart. The eunuch asked Philip to explain a passage from Isaiah 53:7–8, because he needed some more *information*. So beginning with that passage of Scripture, Philip told the man the good news about Jesus. Philip then *invited* the Ethiopian to receive Jesus. Acts 8:38 tells us that Philip went on to baptize the Ethiopian official in some water they found along the road.

We see several gifts of the Holy Spirit operating in this story. There is definitely the gift of evangelism, but there is also the gift of teaching, a word of knowledge, healing, miracles, faith and discernment. It's interesting to note Acts 21:8 reveals that, "Philip the evangelist had four unmarried daughters who prophesied." There was a partnering of evangelism and prophecy in the home of one of the most well-known evangelists in all of Scripture. With that in mind, I believe it should be a normal part of our experience to see the gifts of the Holy Spirit present and operating as we share our faith with others. In our church, we are experiencing the incredible results of seeing evangelism partnered with the gifts of prophecy and healing.

1 Corinthians 14:24–25 (NIV) says, "If an unbeliever or some-one who does not understand comes in while everybody is prophesying, he will be convinced by all that he is a sinner and will be judged by all, and the secrets of his heart will be laid bare. So he will fall down and worship God, exclaiming, 'God is really among you.'" In our church, the use of spiritual gifts is becoming a regular occurrence in our evangelistic efforts. Many times in our services, one of the preachers will hear in his or her spirit that a specific number of people will come to salvation on that day. It's always amazing to later see that exact number of people stand to receive Christ!

We are also learning to be open to the leading of the Holy Spirit, not only inside the walls of our church building but outside the walls as well. As a result of receiving a gentle nudge from the Holy Spirit through a word of knowledge or a word of prophecy, we have seen waitresses, bankers, construction workers, lawyers, teachers and even Walmart shoppers healed and come to salvation. We've adapted the model of Treasure Hunts[2] from Bethel Church in Redding, California, to fit our small town culture. This model involves gathering in small teams to pray and ask the Holy Spirit to show us clues for the treasures God seeks—the people He wants to encourage with a prophetic word, through healing or by bringing them to salvation. We've heard

> **WHEN WE LEARN TO ACTUALLY LISTEN TO WHAT PEOPLE ARE SAYING, WE OFTEN HEAR GOD'S VOICE AND RECEIVE PROPHETIC INSIGHT.**

specific clues such as: *There's a man wearing a red cap standing in the produce section of Walmart whose name is John. This man has extreme back pain.* After the clues were written down, the team goes to Walmart looking for a man in the produce section named

John. Can you imagine how John must have felt when he saw these clues written down from people he didn't know?

Our local leadership sees this partnering of spiritual gifts with evangelism as an increasingly normal part of our day-to-day lives. We've determined to avoid becoming wild-eyed mystics who are divorced from reality and scare more people away than they attract them to Jesus; however, initially it's always a little mysterious to walk up to someone you don't know with a list containing that person's name or a description of them along with a specific area of need or word of prophecy. But in the end, it increases our faith to know the treasure hunt clues were revealed during times of prayer and worship before the team went out. Rarely has our treasure hunt team gone out without seeing people healed, encouraged by a prophetic word or prayed with to receive Jesus. Most people we meet are more than willing to be prayed for once they realize they're the treasure God is seeking. When nonbelievers see ordinary people partnering with an extraordinary God, they're more likely to be open to the gospel of His kingdom. It always amazes us to witness the awesome love of God extended from heaven to people Jesus died for!

It's an awesome thing to hear a word from God. I've learned God's voice sounds different from all the other voices screaming for my attention every minute of the day. God's voice carries the sweet sounds of grace, peace, hope, joy and, especially, love. When we learn to actually listen to what people are saying, we often hear God's voice and receive prophetic insight. And when we speak what we hear using conversational and non-religious language, people are more apt to listen. Think about how Jesus interacted with the woman at the well in John 4. He first listened to her. Then, when He spoke, He did so using normal, everyday words seasoned with courtesy and respect. When Jesus spoke to her of previous husbands, she began to listen more intently. Once Jesus had her attention, He announced He was the Messiah she was waiting for.

My friend, Pastor Bill Leckie, encourages his congregation to fulfill their mission through a three-part vision: *invest, inform* and *invite*.[3] We've adapted those three words in our church to help people discover where they are on their journey to salvation and to connect in membership. We've found people usually have to go through a process of several encounters with God and with His servants before they are ready to come to faith in Jesus and find his or her place in the church.

Here is our adaptation of that three-part vision:

1. **Invest** in people by caring for and meeting needs.

   a. Do not subcontract this out to professionals; rather, make a personal investment.

   b. The vast majority of people who come to salvation do so because someone they know invested time in listening to them and served them personally.

2. **Inform** people of the good news of the gospel with our lives and words.

   a. Be sure to listen to the questions people are actually asking.

   b. Many people just need a little more information before they are ready to receive Christ.

3. **Invite** people to enter into a relationship with Christ and His Church.

   a. Too many Christians are like salesmen who possess a great product or a needed service but never ask for the sale.

   b. Remember, there are many in the valley of decision just waiting for someone to tell them

how to find the Savior. Sometimes all they
need is for someone to invite them.

As I prayed before the service in London, I asked the Lord
to bring someone to salvation that day. On that Sunday morning, I didn't know why I chose the young African woman to role
play with me. But *she* did. She told me she "had a feeling" as she
came into the meeting room that someone would tell her how to
find "this" Jesus she was looking for. Isaiah 30:21 (NIV) reveals
the Lord's desire and intention to direct us: "Whether you turn
to the right or to the left, your ears will hear a voice behind you
saying, 'This is the way; walk in it.'" I've found that being directed
by the Lord involves listening more than anything. I am learning
to quiet the background noise in my life so I can hear the leading
of the Lord ... even when it's just a still, small voice. And through
it all, it's encouraging to remember the Holy Spirit is actively
involved in partnering with us to keep the "e" in our "missions"
so that the whole world may know that Jesus saves.

7

TO PROVIDE ENCOURAGEMENT, EXHORTATION AND COMFORT

Tom Lane

And He Himself gave some to be apostles, some prophets, some evangelists, and some pastors and teachers, for the equipping of the saints for the work of ministry, for the edifying of the body of Christ, till we all come to the unity of the faith and of the knowledge of the Son of God, to a perfect man, to the measure of the stature of the fullness of Christ; that we should no longer be children, tossed to and fro and carried about with every wind of doctrine, by the trickery of men, in the cunning craftiness of deceitful plotting, but, speaking the truth in love, may grow up in all things into Him who is the head—Christ—from whom the whole body, joined and knit together by what every joint supplies, according to the effective working by which every part does its share, causes growth of the body for the edifying of itself in love.

Ephesians 4:11–16 (NKJV)

We live in an unprecedented time in human history. Experts tell us knowledge is doubling every three years, and global information is instantaneously available to us through the Internet, social networking, smart phones, cable/satellite TV and other methods of mass communication. We are truly in an information age.

But there *is* a problem that arises because of this information overload. The sheer amount of information bombarding us every moment of every day can cause stress to our human psyche and lead to confusion as we try to navigate through God's plans for our lives. In addition, the information we receive usually comes from a negative perspective because what sells is negativity, hype and sensationalism! But while they may sell, they also create tremendous confusion, discouragement and depression that produces serious problems in our hearts.

God created us in *His* image; He designed us to live and operate in an atmosphere of faith. In Psalm 100, David instructs us to enter into God's presence with praise and into His courts with thanksgiving. There is an atmosphere of truth, thankfulness and praise in God's presence, and He created us to live and operate in that atmosphere. However, the media-saturated and information age we live in doesn't do much to foster that atmosphere of truth, thankfulness and praise; instead, it creates panic, fear, insinuations, exaggerations, false expectations and accusations. We're constantly surrounded by an atmosphere of unbelief, ingratitude and accusation, which in turn leads to fear, hopelessness, insecurity and stress.

THE GIFT OF PROPHECY IS ONE OF THE GREATEST TOOLS WE HAVE TO CREATE AND PROTECT A GODLY ATMOSPHERE IN OUR LIVES AND IN THE CHURCH.

That's yet another reason why God gives us the gift of prophecy. It's one of the greatest tools we have to create and protect a godly atmosphere in our lives and in the Church. The Apostle Paul wrote to the Corinthian believers they should earnestly desire spiritual gifts, but *especially* the gift of prophecy (1 Corinthians 14:1). He explained the purpose of prophecy was to give edification, exhortation and comfort so they could become the mature believers and functioning Body of Christ God desires.

Our heavenly Father gives His sons and daughters revelations from heaven in order to shed light on the circumstances surrounding them as well as to bring them encouragement and comfort in the midst of those circumstances. These prophetic revelations are some of the best antidotes we have against the negativity that surrounds us. They help us lift our eyes above our circumstances, they renew and strengthen our hope, and they give us confirmations about the path where God is directing us.

However, we don't just live in a negative *world*, our *churches* are also filled with negative influences, criticism and unbelief reinforced by unhealthy prophetic expression. In some churches, prophetic ministry is thought to be God's method of delivering discipline and correction rather than being a tool for building, exhorting and comforting His body. They think prophets are God's messengers to communicate His displeasure, anger and rejection of the individual or the church based on sin or not performing up to the standards of what God expects. With this view of the prophetic, is it any wonder prophetic ministry is limited in its expression or not welcomed in the church at all and people with prophetic gifts are held at arm's-length?

A pastor friend of mine experienced this kind of negativity firsthand in his church. It stemmed from a case of classic Old Testament-style prophetic expression with devastating consequences. Two men associated with his church and who were recognized as having a prophetic gifting announced to the church and its leadership in a worship service that God was displeased and angry. And because of His anger, judgment was imminent. These prophets declared there was idolatry in the house and God was not pleased. Their word was accusatory and demanded a response from the leadership and the church body. They then went on to identify the source of the idolatry—my pastor friend! While I'm well aware none of us are perfect, I have known this man for almost 25 years. He deeply loves God, has a wonderful family and is passionate about doing God's work and leading his church with integrity. However, in spite of all this, fear gripped the church due to the prophetic word delivered by those two men. If God was displeased, what were they to do?

In response to the prophetic message given by these two prophets, the church began a process of bringing correction to the pastor for his idolatry ... even though no specific idolatry was identified! Because the church leadership and the pastor himself could not identify any specific idolatry, they concluded he was deceived and so deceptive in his leadership he was able to completely mask the idolatry. They decided, therefore, they needed to get him help and deliverance for himself and his family. They put him on a leave of absence and sent him and his family to a counseling center so they could all receive counseling and be evaluated on their spiritual health. After three months of extensive ministry and evaluation, it was determined my friend and his family were healthy and not involved with idolatry. The counseling center also determined they were fit for ministry and recommended they reassume their pastoral duties. Yet the stigma of the false prophetic word remained, and it resulted in a multi-year process that ultimately split the church and spawned a very public legal battle for control of the church.

Experiences like this are too often the norm when it comes to the effect of prophetic ministry in the church. With experiences like this, it's no wonder church leadership and individual believers are skeptical of the prophetic. We need God's loving encouragement, direction and comfort; but instead, we receive a finger in our face expressing anger, frustration and rejection supposedly representing how God feels.

The model of prophetic ministry depicted in the New Testament is not like that at all. And it's the New Testament model we are embracing and presenting in this book. God's Word says love believes all things, hopes all things and endures all things. It also says prophecy is for the purpose of building up the body of Christ and all can prophesy. Since the Holy Spirit resides within every believer, God doesn't need prophets to deliver His correction. The Holy Spirit is well able to show us the error of our ways and lead us to repentance. And when prophecy operates in the Church according to the New Testament model, it is edifying, exhorting and comforting (1 Corinthians 14:3)!

As 2003 drew to an end and 2004 was beginning, God launched my wife, Jan, and I into a new ministry assignment at Gateway Church in Dallas/Fort Worth, Texas, after we had spent 22 years on staff serving and ministering at our church in Amarillo, with the last 11 years as co-senior pastor of the church with my best friend. We had been part of the original group who founded the church in Amarillo and had been members there for 27 years. I mention all that to say this was a *major* change in direction and ministry for us.

As God began speaking to us about this change of direction, we knew we needed His clear direction and confirmation. In the early days of 2004, a prophet came to minister at the church. Although he knew no specific details before he came, he came with a clear word of change. He first gave a word to my best friend and co-senior pastor about the change

WE ALL NEED AND WANT GOD'S CONFIRMATION AND DIRECTION RELATING TO THE EVENTS OF OUR LIVES.

in ministry relationship he saw developing between the two of us and inquired as to what was happening between us and with the leadership of the church. Then, he singled out Jan and me in a worship service and told us: "There is an open door in 2004, so walk through the door." He went on to tell us God's hand was upon us and He would anoint us in a new way in this new season. Wow, what a confirmation of the change taking place in our life! It resulted in every effect Scripture attributes to prophetic ministry—it was encouraging to us, it confirmed God's direction to us and built our faith, and it gave us peace in the midst of all the emotions associated with the change. God's commitment to us and our desire to know and do His will opened the door for the prophetic encouragement to be received.

The scope of the situation doesn't matter—it could be simple or life-changing—the reality is we *all* need and want God's confirmation and direction relating to the events of our lives. When my daughter, Lisa, was a freshman in college, she lived away from home. Lisa's heart was tender and turned toward God. Her desire was to know and do God's will for her life. She also had a great desire to be a wife and a mom, which she had seen modeled in our family by Jan. When Jan and I took a trip to visit Lisa and meet the young man she was dating, it didn't seem like he had the same love and passion for God as Lisa had. This handsome young man had already graduated from college and was working. He was passionately pursuing our daughter but wasn't so passionate in his pursuit of God. As Lisa's parents, this caused us great concern. One morning as I was praying and writing in my journal, I focused my prayers on Lisa. (As a normal part of my daily prayer times, I pray for Jan and each of my kids. It's something I've done for more than 28 years.) As I prayed to the Lord and expressed my concern about her developing relationship with the young man, the Lord spoke to me and said: "Tell Lisa if she will not compromise, I am preparing the husband of her dreams." The clarity of the word caused me to pause and evaluate the full implication of the word. Was that me or was it God? As I processed and prayed, I

GENUINE PROPHETIC WORDS FROM THE HEART OF GOD CAN COME FROM PARENTS, CO-WORKERS, FRIENDS AND STRANGERS, BUT THEY WILL ALWAYS HAVE THE EFFECT OF ENCOURAGEMENT, CONFIRMING DIRECTION AND BRINGING COMFORT IN OUR LIVES.

expressed my opinion to God: "This particular guy must not be the guy You are preparing for Lisa, because not only does he not meet *my* qualifications, but he doesn't meet yours either, right Lord?" God made no further comment. That was all I got ... just that simple statement of promise. But it was so clear and unexpected, I knew it was God.

A short time later, I told Lisa I had been praying for her and God spoke to me. Lisa knew I prayed for her. I had always openly prayed for her and with her as she grew up, so my statement didn't surprise her. Instead, in a way that was so typical of her heart toward me and God, she responded: "Really Dad, what did He say?" I gave her the word as God had given it to me: "Honey, I heard God tell me to tell you that if you won't compromise, He is preparing the husband of your dreams." I wanted to say more. I wanted to add my interpretation to the simple statement like,

"And God is not preparing *this* guy as the husband of your dreams!" But I didn't. I left it at that, because I knew when we receive a word from God, we must be careful not to give our interpretation or add to it: God can interpret His own messages far better than we can.

Pretty soon after that, Lisa ended her relationship with the guy she had been dating. Over the next three years, she occasionally asked me to remind her about what God had spoken that day in my prayer time, and I would restate the message. Sometimes, because I had written it down in my journal, I'd pull out the journal and turn to the page where I recorded the word from God and show her what I wrote. So imagine our joy when she met a godly young man named Braxton at a holiday party hosted by the young adults at our church. Braxton had been involved with our young adult ministry for a while, and his passion for God was as fervent as Lisa's.

As Lisa and Braxton's dating relationship began, God spoke to both Jan and I individually and told us this was the man He had been preparing for Lisa. We watched in marvel and wonder as their relationship developed. Like Mary, the mother of Jesus, we held these words from God in our hearts until the day when Lisa told us Braxton wanted to have a "talk" with me. As we talked over a Coke, Braxton asked me for Lisa's hand in marriage. That's when I was able to tell him (and then later both of them) the whole story of God's word given to us and how He had been at work in the development of their relationship for many years.

It all began with a prophetic word God spoke in prayer. It was a word of encouragement, a word of confirmation and direction and a word that brought peace and comfort. Not all prophetic words need to be given in a worship service or by a vocational minister. Genuine prophetic words from the heart of God can come from parents, co-workers, friends and strangers, but they will *always* have the effect of encouragement, confirming direction and bringing comfort in our lives.

The Bible tells us the testimony of Jesus is the spirit of prophecy (Revelation 19:10). Do you need a message of good news? In this negative and discouraging world filled with alarmingly bad news and emotionally gripping information coming at us 24/7, do you need to be encouraged, receive direction and confirmation from God for circumstances in your life or be comforted through some situation you're facing? The gospel of Jesus is *good* news! Every once in a while—more often than we might realize or acknowledge—we need to be reminded of that fact. It's good news that our sins are forgiven! It's good news that a way has been made for us to restore our relationship with God through Jesus Christ's righteousness and not our own. It's good news that God knows the specific details of our every situation. And it's good news that He is *always* at work to fulfill His plans in our lives.

Misconceptions
of
Prophetic Ministry

GOD'S ONLY METHOD
OF COMMUNICATION
IS THROUGH SCRIPTURE

Tom Lane

I was at lunch one day with a local pastor friend of mine. Both of our churches were large enough that they had a sphere of influence in our city that extended beyond the location of our neighborhoods. Although our theology didn't match step for step, we shared a common personal relationship with Jesus Christ, a mutual respect for each other and a deep desire to help people. As we talked over lunch, our conversation eventually turned to how God works and reveals Himself in people's lives.

We specifically talked about how God speaks to people, and after some lively, friendly discussion, he announced to me, "I don't believe God speaks like you believe He speaks!" To which I responded, "Yes, you do!" This led to a tennis-like volley of words between us. He'd respond, "No, I don't!" and I would assure him he did. Like two kids in an argument on the playground, we went back and forth with each other: "Yes, you do." ... "No, I don't!" ... "Yes, you do!" Finally, I said, "OK, I'll prove to you that we believe the same." I then asked him: "When you're studying for your sermon, does God speak to you?" "Yes," he replied, "He speaks through His Word." I said, "That's right, He speaks to you through His Word, but then you deliver the message, and as you present the message God's given you, He personally speaks to people in a miraculous way, right? He speaks something to their hearts, asking them at times to make a response to His word through the ministry of preaching, isn't that true?" "Yes," he replied again. "So," I said, "God speaks to people and gives them information through your message that may lead them to make a response. We know it's Him because it's consistent with the principles outlined in the Bible, don't you agree?" Cautiously, he responded, "Y–e–s," like he was about to be led into a trap. I assured him, "Like you, I don't believe God speaks any new revelation today or in any direction that's not consistent with His revealed Word that's recorded and reflected in the Bible. So, we believe God speaks the same way. See, I told you we believed the same." I then went on to say:

WHEN WE LACK INSIGHT INTO OUR CIRCUMSTANCES AND DON'T UNDERSTAND WHAT TO DO NEXT, WE NEED GOD TO SPEAK TO US.

"I simply believe God preaches messages *all the time*, not just when we're in the pulpit. I believe He speaks in a variety of ways, but when He speaks, it is *never* inconsistent with His nature or the principles of His Word."

Some of my pastoral friends have tried to convince me we need no further revelation because Jesus was the full revelation of God. They tell me He is the Word, and the Word became flesh and dwelt among us, and through Him we have all we need. They say Paul even wrote about it in his letter to the Corinthians:

For we know in part and we prophesy in part; but when the perfect comes, the partial will be done away. When I was a child, I used to speak like a child, think like a child, reason like a child; when I became a man, I did away with childish things. For now we see in a mirror dimly, but then face to face; now I know in part, but then I will know fully just as I also have been fully known. But now faith, hope, love, abide these three; but the greatest of these is love.

1 Corinthians 13:9–13 (NASB)

I completely agree with my friends that Paul was talking about Jesus Christ in this passage of Scripture. I just think Paul was talking about when Jesus returns to earth to receive His bride ... not His time on earth living as a man. Paul's analogies of a child becoming a man and of seeing through a mirror dimly only work if they're viewed in context of Christ's second coming. At His second coming, I will be made perfect, I will see perfectly, and I will know everything even as He knows. But I don't have that knowledge today. I still need Him to speak to me, lead me and show me all He wants me to do for Him.

What's really cool about this issue of God speaking is that Jesus even talked about it with His disciples:

"I am the good shepherd, and I know My own and My own know Me, even as the Father knows Me and I know the Father; and I lay down My life for the sheep. I have other sheep, which are not of this fold; I must bring them also, and they will hear My voice; and they will become one flock with one shepherd."

John 10:14–16 (NASB)

Jesus declared He would speak to His sheep and His sheep would know His voice and follow Him. So how do we know His voice? Jesus said we'd know His voice because the Holy Spirit would be with us. He gave us these comforting words to ease our concerns and fears:

"But I tell you the truth, it is to your advantage that I go away; for if I do not go away, the Helper will not come to you; but if I go, I will send Him to you."

John 16:7 (NASB)

Life can be so hard and circumstances so critical that knowing the right way to proceed is more than a matter of preference; it is *essential*. There are countless circumstances, opportunities and relationships that continuously demand our attention. Knowing exactly what to do, when to do it and the right method to employ as we implement solutions requires heavenly wisdom. When we lack insight into our circumstances and don't understand what to do next, we need God to speak to us. When we need direction relating to difficult circumstances and confirmation relating to God's work, direction and timing, we need a word of wisdom. And sometimes, we just need encouragement from God about a specific situation, its purpose and God's present work in it. We need to be assured of His care for us.

In Proverbs 2:6 (NASB), Solomon wrote: "For *the Lord gives wisdom*; from His mouth come knowledge and understanding." And James wrote:

*Consider it all joy, my brethren, when you encounter various trials, knowing that the testing of your faith produces endurance. And let endurance have its perfect result, so that you may be perfect and complete, lacking in nothing. But **if any of you lacks wisdom, let him ask of God**, who gives to all generously and without reproach, and it will be given to him. But he must ask in faith without any doubting, for the one who doubts is like the surf of the sea, driven and tossed by the wind. For that man ought not to expect that he will receive anything from the Lord, being a double-minded man, unstable in all his ways.*

James 1:2–8 (NASB, emphasis added)

One Saturday evening during a worship service, the Lord drew my attention to a woman standing in the back row of the auditorium. I watched her as worship continued, and the Lord spoke to my heart. He said, "Tell her that the opportunity is from My hand, and if she'll say yes, I will be with her and help her in her new assignment. Tell her she'll be blessed if she'll respond because this opportunity is from Me."

When the Lord speaks like this to me, it's not in an audible voice; it's an impression in my inner conscience. Usually (but not always), it's for someone I've never met and it's regarding circumstances about which I know nothing. I believe the Holy Spirit living in me brings this information to my awareness and wants to use me as His representative to deliver the word to that particular individual.

That's exactly the way it was in this instance. As worship came to a close, I stepped forward and announced that I had a word from the Lord for a lady in the back row. I described her while I made eye contact with her, and she acknowledged that she knew I was talking with her. I didn't know the lady, and as far as I knew, we had never met. I told her the word the Lord gave me for her was: "If you say yes to this opportunity that I have given you, then I will be with you and help you in your new assignment." I went on to tell her that the Lord wanted her to know she would be

IF WE LIMIT GOD'S ABILITY TO SPEAK TO US ONLY THROUGH SCRIPTURE, WE MISS DIVINE OPPORTUNITIES FOR SPECIFIC WISDOM, DIRECTION AND COMFORT TO BE REVEALED THROUGH THE HOLY SPIRIT'S WORK.

blessed if she'd walk through this open door because the opportunity was from Him. I then concluded by asking her if what I was sharing made sense to her. She nodded in affirmation as the congregation clapped, and we transitioned the service into the welcome time and then went into the message.

When the service was over, the woman came forward to talk with me and seemed anxious to get my attention. She began our conversation by asking: "What was that?" I thought: *Oh great, the word was off base, and I embarrassed her* (which is something I *never* want to do when I give a word to someone). I answered by saying, "Well that's what the Bible calls a prophetic word, and it's something we believe God gives to people in order to bring direction, encouragement and comfort. How do you feel about that prophetic word?" She said, "Oh my gosh, how did you know?" And I said, "I didn't know! I mean, I don't know what the word means, but I assume it's a message from God to help you. Can you share with me what it means?"

She told me the previous Friday, before she left the office for the weekend, she had been offered a promotion. However, she felt completely unqualified to fill the position and had been wrestling all weekend on whether to take the promotion or decline it. She said, "They're expecting my decision when I go back to work on Monday." Then she told me she was a first-time visitor to our church. She was in awe of how God spoke to her need for a decision on the open door before her

GOD REVEALS HIMSELF TO US THROUGH A VARIETY OF METHODS. HIS WORK IS ALL AROUND US.

and was amazed at how specific His answer was for her situation. She then told me she had come to the service anxious and in need of an answer from God, and now she was leaving with clear direction and a deep sense of peace about the promotion she had been offered.

I've discovered God wants to be far more involved in all the circumstances of our lives than we are willing to involve Him. Day in and day out, we face so many decisions (like the one this woman was facing) that can't be answered directly with a specific chapter or verse from the Bible. However, we still want and need to know God's wisdom and direction for the circumstances we face. If we limit God's ability to speak to us only through Scripture, we miss divine opportunities for specific wisdom, direction and comfort to be revealed through the Holy Spirit's work.

When I'm in a group of people, I'm not typically overwhelmed with prophetic words for people. But almost without exception, if I pause in any situation and ask God to speak, I will get an impression or a word. Over the years, I've learned to test those impressions and words I receive just as I would if I were about to deliver it in a public setting. I ask myself if it meets the three-fold criteria of being edifying, exhorting and comforting. If the answer is yes, then I ask if I have a platform for giving the word. Timing is everything. This is true in the physical realm, and it's true in the spiritual realm as well. When I've received a word that meets the three-fold test, but I don't have a legitimate platform for delivering the word, I hold onto the word and don't share it.

So what do I mean by legitimate platform? I ask myself if I can naturally give the word without it interrupting something and creating an awkward situation. Would I have to usurp the authority of the moment to give the word to the individual or the group? If so, I don't give the word. I believe God is a perfect gentleman, and as His representative, I need to consider the timing of the delivery as much as the content and method of delivering the word. If there's not opportunity in the moment, then I pray the word I've received into the situation and hold it until it would be appropriate to express it. If an opportunity doesn't present itself for me to express the word publicly, then I assume God has simply given me some specific insight for the purpose of prayer. As God's servants, we are to represent Him and partner with Him in all we do ... not seek to create a platform for expanding our reputation at His expense. Paul spoke to this when he said: "The spirits of prophets are subject to the control of prophets" (1 Corinthians 14:32, NIV).

Not long ago, I was at an airport sitting at the gate waiting to board a flight. As I scanned the other passengers, my eyes caught a woman seated in the same gate area as me. She was curled up in the seat with a book, and it seemed like she had been there a while. I thought to myself: *she looks like she's home in her family room with her robe and slippers on, a cup of coffee in hand and sitting by a fire reading her favorite book.* As my attention focused on her, I got a clear impression I knew was from the Lord related to the purpose of her travel. As I mulled over the content of what I was receiving, I asked the Lord what I was supposed to do with this information. Do I go over and interrupt her cozy moment? I had already tested it to make sure what I was sensing passed the three-fold test of encouraging, exhorting and comforting. Also, I was ready and willing to take the risk and give the word to the lady even if she thought I was a little wacky, but I didn't have a legitimate platform. So I prayed and asked the Lord to create one for me if He wanted me to give the word to this lady. The seats next to her were filled, so my first thought was God could create a legitimate platform by having one of the people around her move and leave a seat open where I could sit and have an opportunity to share the word. When that didn't happen, I thought we might be seated next to each other on the flight and that would create a platform for delivering the word, but that didn't happen either. Finally, I thought maybe there might be an opportunity at the baggage claim to strike up a conversation with her that would provide a legitimate platform to give her the word, but that opportunity never materialized.

I could have walked up to her and created my own platform to give her the word. And while there are times when the Lord may lead that way, I think we must be cautious and wait to be clearly directed before doing something bold to create a platform. When a legitimate platform doesn't exist, your default should be to wait to deliver the word. Timing is everything! So even though I believe the word I received was insight from the Lord, I feel like it wasn't mine to deliver. Instead, it was my responsibility to pray for her. I think this is what Paul meant when he described the working partnership and ministry that took place between Apollos and himself:

"I planted, Apollos watered, but God gave the growth. So neither he who plants nor he who waters is anything, but only God who gives the growth. He who plants and he who waters are one, and each will receive his wages according to his *labor. For we are God's fellow workers. You are God's field, God's building."*

1 Corinthians 3:6–9, ESV.

God reveals Himself to us through a variety of methods. His work is all around us. If we're willing to let Him speak to us, He is faithful to protect us from being led into error. He is always consistent. He is the same yesterday, today and forever. He is not fickle or moody. He never wakes up in a bad mood. And He doesn't experience Doctor Jekyll and Mr. Hyde kind of changes in His personality. You can rest assured that *every* one of His words of revelation will *always* be consistent with His nature and character, which the Bible clearly portrays for us to see, learn and know.

God is still speaking today. Are you tuned in and open to the things He is saying?

9

PROPHETS ARE GOD'S
WATCHMEN ON THE WALL

Tom Lane

⸻

There are numerous accounts throughout the Old Testament showcasing the wayward tendencies of God's people. Because of mankind's habitual tendency to stray from their relationship with God, He appointed prophets to be His voice to the people. God set them to be His watchmen over His people, and they served as God's overseers and enforcers of man's performance under the covenant between God and man.

WATCHMEN ON THE WALL

So where did this "watchmen on the wall" mentality come from? It's rooted in the Old Testament model of prophetic ministry and the living conditions of the day. The people lived in cities made secure from enemy attack by the strong walls surrounding the city. The watchmen stood as lookouts to identify danger and warn against enemy attack. Isaiah 62:6 (ESV) says, "On your walls, O Jerusalem, I have set watchmen; all the day and all the night they shall never be silent."

From this perspective of protection, watchmen were appointed for the work of God. 2 Kings 11:18 (ESV) says: "Then all the people of the land went to the house of Baal and tore it down; his altars and his images they broke in pieces, and they killed Mattan the priest of Baal before the altars. And the priest posted watchmen over the house of the Lord." God gave the prophet Ezekiel one of these assignments: "Son of man, I have made you a watchman for the house of Israel; therefore hear a word from My mouth, and give them warning from Me" (Ezekiel 3:17, NKJV).

God has always desired to communicate with His children in an intimate and personal way. Like a loving father, He wants to interact with His children and guide them in the way they should go. We see this first demonstrated in His relationship with Adam and Eve in the Garden of Eden. The Bible says God walked with Adam and Eve in the cool of the day, but sin changed Adam and Eve's desire to talk with God face to face (Genesis 3:8–9). The shame of their sin led them to cover themselves and hide from God.

In the same way, the children of Israel asked Moses to talk with God on their behalf and relay His message to them:

Now when all the people saw the thunder and the flashes of lightning and the sound of the trumpet and the mountain smoking, the people were afraid and trembled, and they stood far off and said to Moses, "You speak to us, and we will listen; but do not let God speak to us, lest we die."

Exodus 20:18–19 (ESV)

God chose to honor their request by speaking to them through Moses as they journeyed through the wilderness. This paradigm continued throughout the Old Testament. The ministry of God to His people was relegated to only a few chosen individuals. God spoke to His people through appointed leaders like the judges as well as selected representatives like Samuel, Jonah and a host of other prophets, because He chose to respect the people's desire for Him not to talk with them face to face.

There have been many over the years who have mistakenly used similar scripture passages and stories from the Old Testament to support their perspective that God continues to need men and women to serve as enforcers of His covenant with men. They view prophets through an Old Testament lens and believe prophets still serve as watchmen mistrustfully looking out for infractions by God's people and their spiritual leaders. But this Old Testament model doesn't fit with the relational model demonstrated throughout the New Testament.

For 27 years, I served in various leadership and staff capacities at Trinity Fellowship Church in Amarillo, Texas, before coming to Gateway Church in 2004. In the early 1980s, while Trinity Fellowship was still in its early years and at a formative stage in its development, there was a member in our congregation who asked to meet with the elders. He said he had something important from the Lord to share with the elders, and he wanted the entire body of elders to hear it at the same time so they could process it together. He told us he felt it was impor-

> **GOD HAS ALWAYS DESIRED TO COMMUNICATE WITH HIS CHILDREN IN AN INTIMATE AND PERSONAL WAY. LIKE A LOVING FATHER, HE WANTS TO INTERACT WITH HIS CHILDREN AND GUIDE THEM IN THE WAY THEY SHOULD GO.**

tant for him to share the word with the whole elder body at the same time rather than sharing with me or another leader before meeting with the elders. Giving in to his demand was a rookie mistake on my part. What I know today is this: If a prophet will not submit his word before he gives the word, it is a clear indication he's not submitted to the leadership of the church. An unwillingness to submit the word for processing actually invalidates the delivery as coming from God and renders the word illegitimate regardless of the content. Out of our collective inexperience and sincere desire to embrace all God had for our church, we accommodated his request and set up a time to meet with him without processing it first beforehand. We all felt a degree of cautiousness, but he was a committed member who regularly attended, gave and was involved, so we were willing to hear what he had to say. When we met with him, he announced to us God had designated him to be a prophet to our body of believers. He believed God had appointed him to be a "watchman on the wall." He explained how God had given him this assignment and told us it was vital for us to accept him in this role in order for the work God wanted to do through the church to take place in its full measure.

Because Trinity Fellowship is a church that embraces all the gifts of the Holy Spirit as an expression of His work to exalt Jesus, his statement didn't fall outside the bounds of our ministry perspective. The pastors and elders at Trinity Fellowship have always been earnestly focused on hearing and obeying God, so a word of this nature was taken very seriously. We discussed his declaration that God had appointed him as our "prophet" from a perspective of believing in the gifts of the Spirit operating in

WHEN PROPHETIC MINISTRY ISN'T CONNECTED IN PARTNERSHIP WITH THE LEADERSHIP OF A CHURCH, IT ENDS UP BEING NOTHING MORE THAN ADVERSARIAL NITPICKING.

the church and with a desire to hear and embrace God's direction in all that's involved with leading the church. As we processed through all of this, we concluded there were at least two issues pointing to the fact that what he told us wasn't a word from God for us. Our response to him was as kind as it could be, and yet, we were also very clear so he wouldn't wonder where we stood or misread our response. We first told him we didn't believe God needed "watchmen on the wall" to mistrustfully observe the church in anticipation of our failure. But then we acknowledged he might have a prophetic gift and might even be a prophet to some other body; we just didn't believe he functioned in that role in relation to us and our church.

We wanted our communication to be clear to him. The rationale behind our conclusion was two-fold: First, there was an attitude of mistrust that seemed to underlie his self-appointment. Although he was a member of the church, he didn't hold any kind of position of recognized leadership. We felt if God were to appoint a person to the office of prophet in our church, it wouldn't be from the perspective of a "watchman on the wall," and it would be someone who was a recognized leader working alongside other leaders in a collective effort to fulfill God's work. We believe a prophet, as a minister in the church, is part of a team of leaders who are submitted to each other and accountable to one another.

Second, we felt his declaration implied there was only one appointed person to receive and then deliver God's word of revelation or confirm God's direction to the church. We fundamentally disagreed with this view of God's way of leading the church and, more specifically, with this view of the role of prophetic ministry in the church. We felt his word implied we might not hear God correctly without him as our prophet or, even worse, we might make mistakes that would disqualify us from God's blessing and work among us. Although both of those possibilities exist in any ministry, we didn't feel it was God's plan for the ministry of the prophet and for prophetic ministry to function within the church from a position that was independent and relationally outside of the church's leadership. A prophet is still under the command of Jesus to love (John 13:34), so how could his ministry in the church and to the leadership of the church be based on a foundation of mistrust? We also didn't believe the prophetic office and prophetic ministry specifically existed to be the sole protector from all danger and error which might occur in the church. The prophetic office and prophetic ministry exist to build the church, and prophetic individuals need to participate in its leadership.

When we communicated our response to the man, he took an adversarial position toward us. He accused us of resisting God and closing ourselves off from God's direction to protect our leadership position. He predicted judgment and dire consequences would result from our decision. This is, coincidentally, another error often associated with prophetic ministry. Behind the ministry of some prophets lies the erroneous assumption that a rejection of the prophet or his message is a rejection of God. This error has led to many abuses perpetrated upon the Church by individuals, and it has given prophetic ministry and the prophetic gift a bad name in the Church. The reality is, however, this perspective of prophetic ministry can't be fully supported in Scripture when viewed through the lens of the New Testament's model of prophetic ministry and its impact on the Church. God's Word instructs us to test the spirits to see if they are from God (1 John 4:1). It also tells us prophetic ministry exists to build up, exhort and comfort both the individual and the Church body as a whole (1 Corinthians 14:3), which is a far cry from the spirit of correction and independence that often accompanies prophetic ministry today.

AT ARM'S LENGTH

Does prophetic ministry need to be independent from a relational connection with the Church and its leaders in order to be a valid expression of God? Some would say yes due to the fact it can become sympathetic to the weaknesses and sins of the leaders it's relationally connected with, and then the message and purpose of the prophetic is compromised. Do prophets really need to stand outside the body of Christ and shout their words of direction and judgment for their ministry to remain uncompromised and therefore a valid expression from God? But where do you find a unity of the body and its leadership in that model? Aren't we to be one even as He is one?

When prophetic ministry isn't connected in partnership with the leadership of a church, it ends up being nothing more than adversarial nitpicking. From this adversarial perspective, the prophet feels responsible to serve as God's corrective agent for pastors, leaders and congregants who (through prophetic ministry) are accused of displeasing God and going astray in their service to Him. Because of their negative critical tone, the message and ministry of these prophets are met with direct and subtle resistance. Is it any wonder then that church leaders take a defensive posture toward prophets and their ministry with this kind of adversarial and negative approach? It also explains why those who operate under this misdirected model feel so ostracized from the church. Out of a sense of exclusion, many of these prophets congregate in their own communities outside the church, feeling completely excluded and rejected from the body of Christ in general.

> **THE HOLY SPIRIT MINISTERS TO GOD'S CHILDREN BY LEADING, GUIDING, TEACHING, COMFORTING AND EMPOWERING THEM FOR LIFE AND SERVICE TO GOD.**

From the safety of their prophetic communities, they hurl accusations like terrorists launching raids on innocent communities of believers called the Church. They're attempting to control with fear through the words they deliver. Through a message of displeasure with the Church and its leaders, they demand corrective action through repentance "or else." Sometimes these spiritual terrorists actually come into the church uninvited, in defiance to the leaders' authority, and deliver their message in a worship service or gathering with an intentionally embarrassing and destructive effect. They feel empowered by God and justified to act on His behalf, because they feel it's their God-appointed mission to resist "apostate leaders" and their "wayward leadership" of God's people by exercising their prophetic control upon the church.

THE PRESENT MINISTRY OF THE HOLY SPIRIT

Jesus told the disciples it was to their advantage that He leave them and return to the Father. He knew that following His departure, He would send the Holy Spirit to them:

> *Nevertheless, I tell you the truth: it is to your advantage that I go away, for if I do not go away, the Helper will not come to you. But if I go, I will send him to you. And when he comes, he will convict the world concerning sin and righteousness and judgment: concerning sin, because they do not believe in me; concerning righteousness, because I go to the Father, and you will see me no longer; concerning judgment, because the ruler of this world is judged.*
>
> **John 16:7–11 (ESV)**

It seems clear the Holy Spirit's presence in each believer's life fills the role previously held by the prophets, judges and God's appointed leaders. Under the new covenant, the prophet no longer functions as God's appointed representative to bring direction and correction to His people. The Holy Spirit has been given the ministry of translating God's word to His people. And although He uses men to help deliver His message and apply His message to their lives and circumstances, it is solely the Holy Spirit's work to bring conviction and correction. Jesus told the disciples He would send the Holy Spirit, and when the Holy Spirit came, He would convict the world of sin, righteousness and judgment (John 16:7–11). The Holy Spirit ministers to God's children by leading, guiding, teaching, comforting and empowering them for life and service to God (John 14:26; John 15:26–27; Acts 1:8).

Through our new covenant in Jesus, we have been made righteous. God has poured out His wrath toward sin on Jesus and given us forgiveness, righteousness and an intimate relationship with Him through the ministry of the Holy Spirit.

The empowering work of the Holy Spirit is to build up the body of Christ. The gifts of the Spirit, including prophecy, are ministry tools for helping, encouraging and comforting individuals in the work of God. The positive nature of New Testament prophetic ministry makes it a necessary tool in our ministry arsenal. Paul encouraged the Corinthian church to embrace prophetic minis- try. He also encouraged them to earnestly desire spiritual gifts, but especially that they would prophesy (1 Corinthians 14:1). He then went on to say the purpose of prophecy is to give edifica- tion, exhortation and comfort (1 Corinthians 14:3). There is not a place for a "watchman on the wall" any longer! There is no longer a need for a watchman. The Holy Spirit now fills that role! That model went away with the old covenant and has been replaced with a better one in the new covenant. Praise God!

> *Unless the Lord builds the house, those who build it labor in vain. Unless the Lord watches over the city, the watchman stays awake in vain.*
>
> **Psalm 127:1 (ESV)**

10

PROPHECY IS NOT FOR TODAY

Wayne Drain

For in him you have been enriched in every way—with all kinds of speech and with all knowledge—God thus confirming our testimony about Christ among you. Therefore you do not lack any spiritual gift as you eagerly wait for our Lord Jesus Christ to be revealed.

1 Corinthians 1:5–7 (NIV)

Many wonder if God still speaks into the lives of people today. As a pastor, I am often asked questions such as: Does God still speak to His people today? Does God still heal people? Are the gifts of the Spirit still in operation?

I once heard a well-meaning pastor who was doing a series on 1 Corinthians say in a message, "Anyone who believes in the Baptism of the Holy Spirit is deceived and doesn't understand the word of God!" Another time, I heard a different church leader say, "Speaking in tongues and giving prophecies are demonic manifestations!"

Just about any time someone brings up something about the Holy Spirit or spiritual gifts, there's more often than not a myriad of questions and opinions that accompany it! Endless books have been written dealing with questions about the Holy Spirit ranging from one extreme to the other. It amazes me that the Holy Spirit—the one whom Jesus sent to come alongside us, guide us into all truth and empower us to be His witnesses—is so widely misunderstood.

In this chapter, we're going to take a closer look at an unfortunate misconception many Christians hold—the belief that spiritual gifts—including prophecy—are not for today.

There are two basic views held among Christian believers about spiritual gifts. Both sides agree that the miraculous gifts were given by the Holy Spirit on the Day of Pentecost. However, one group believes there is no longer a need for these gifts since the apostolic age has ended with the death of the Apostle John and the canon of Scripture is complete. These folks are called Cessationists. In Christian theology, Cessationism is the view that miraculous gifts of the Holy Spirit, such as tongues, prophecy and healing, ceased to be practiced early on in church history. The alternate view is these miraculous gifts of the Holy Spirit have been available for use by the Church ever since the Day of Pentecost (Acts 2:1–4, 39). This group is often referred to as Continuationists. Cessationists hold that there's no need for the expression of these gifts because no miracles are performed by God today. Continuationists, on the other hand, disagree and believe the gifts of the Holy Spirit are as relevant today as they were in the time of the early saints in the book of Acts. While it's true there seems to

PROPHECY IS SIMPLY GOD MAKING HIS WORD ALIVE AND REAL IN REGARDS TO A SPECIFIC SITUATION. NO AUTHENTIC PROPHECY WILL EVER CONTRADICT SCRIPTURE.

have been a diminishing of these gifts after the apostolic age, I believe this wasn't because the Lord withdrew them. Instead, to quote John Wesley, it was because "the love of many, almost of all

Christians, so called, was 'waxed cold' ... This was the real cause why the extraordinary gifts of the Holy Ghost were no longer to be found in the Christian church."

The passage most often used to justify the belief that spiritual gifts are not for today is 1 Corinthians 13:8–13:

> *Love never fails. But where there are prophecies, they will cease; where there are tongues, they will be stilled; where there is knowledge, it will pass away. For we know in part and we prophesy in part, but when perfection comes, the imperfect disappears. When I was a child, I talked like a child, I thought like a child, I reasoned like a child. When I became a man, I put childish ways behind me. Now we see but a poor reflection as in a mirror; then we shall see face to face. Now I know in part; then I shall know fully, even as I am fully known. And now these three remain: faith, hope and love. But the greatest of these is love.*

A large segment of the church believes the "perfection" here refers to the Scriptures themselves. But I don't believe it refers to the age we're currently living in, because this passage plainly refers to a time in the future "when perfection comes." My opinion is the "perfection" spoken of in this passage has to do with the return of Jesus, when we will see Him face to face. The phrase "see face to face" is used several times in the Old Testament, and while it doesn't refer to seeing God fully (for no finite creature can ever do that), it nonetheless refers to seeing God personally and truly. A number of respected theologians have clearly concluded the "when" in verse 10 is referring to the return of Jesus:

> *"The key issue is what time is meant by the word when in verse 10: 'When the perfect is come, the imperfect will pass away.' Some who hold that these gifts have ceased believe this phrase refers to a time earlier than the time of the Lord's return, such as when the Church is mature or when Scripture is complete. However, the meaning of verse 12 seems to*

indicate this phrase is speaking about the time of the Lord's return. So when Paul says, 'but then face to face,' he clearly means, but then we shall see God face to face."[1]

Wayne Grudem

"The whole passage strongly proves that we should expect spiritual gifts to remain right up till the end of this age because their divine purpose will not be achieved until perfection comes. There is nothing in Scripture, reason, or experience to make us believe that the gifts of the Spirit are not for today—every one of them."[2]

Donald Gee

So when Paul says, "then we shall see face to face," he clearly means a time that is yet to come when we will "see his face, and his name will be on their foreheads" (Revelation 22:4). Indeed, that will be the greatest blessing of heaven and our greatest joy for all eternity.

The whole point of 1 Corinthians 13:8–13 is to show us love is superior to gifts such as prophecy because those gifts will one day pass away, but love will never pass away. So when Paul was referring to the "imperfect" in verse 10, he was not only including prophecy but all the other gifts such as "tongues" and "knowledge," which will eventually pass away (1 Corinthians 13:8). It stands to reason though, based on Paul's words in Romans 11:29, that these wonderful gifts would not be taken away before Christ's return: "The gifts and callings of God are without repentance." Another truth that cannot be ignored comes from the writer of Hebrews 13:8: "Jesus Christ is the same yesterday, today and forever."

So if you were to ask me, "What about prophecy? Is prophecy for today?" Without a doubt, I would respond with a resounding, "Yes! Prophecy *is* for today." Prophecy is simply God making His word alive and real in regards to a specific situation. No authentic prophecy will ever contradict Scripture. If it does, that would be a "false prophecy" and it should be judged as such (1 Corinthians 4:29).

One of the many things that amazes me about our awesome God is that He puts His treasure in earthen vessels. God doesn't take away the gifts He gives due to our immaturity; rather, the Holy Spirit is continually teaching believers directly and raising up grace gifts within us to equip and mature God's people.

I once heard Pastor Jimmy Evans say, "Prophecy proves God." From my own experience, I heartily agree. I can tell you prophecy *does* take place today and is very helpful. Let me give you an example I witnessed personally. On a Sunday morning, as I was about to share a message with my congregation, I noticed a lady walk into the back of the auditorium and sit down. I didn't recognize her. But when I looked at her face, I felt a strong impression in my spirit to say to her, "The thing you are thinking about doing is not from the Lord. Jesus came to give life."

I was hesitant to say this, especially because this lady was a visitor and possibly unfamiliar with prophecy. I tried to start my sermon, but the impression only grew stronger. So I took a minute to explain what prophecy is and then spoke the word I had received. The lady seemed visibly moved. She rose from her chair and began walking toward the front. Weeping as she came forward, she asked to share her story, and I felt I should allow her to. That very morning, she had discovered her husband was leaving her for another woman. Being distraught, she put her affairs in order and left the house intending to commit suicide by driving her car off a boat ramp into the Arkansas River. The route from her home to the river required that she

MATURE BELIEVERS NEED TO CAREFULLY WEIGH PROPHETIC WORDS, AND PROPHECIES SHOULD ALWAYS BE GIVEN IN A FITTING AND ORDERLY WAY.

drive past our building. As she did, she felt an irresistible urge to pull into our church's parking lot. As she sat there in her car, she cried out that there must not be a God. She then heard a voice inside her say: *Go into this church and a man will speak My words to you.* She testified that she was still here because God had spoken to her through prophecy. Today, this woman is alive and serving as a Sunday school teacher in her church. If asked if prophecy is for today, I'm reasonably sure she would answer, "Yes ... without a doubt!"

Last year, there were numerous deaths in America caused by car wrecks, but that doesn't mean we should stop driving cars. It just means we should drive safely, stay alert and abide by the laws. I have seen outrageous abuses of prophecy used to manipulate, control or gain power in the lives of immature or gullible believers and non-believers alike. There have also been abuses by teachers, pastors and evangelists who have taught error and led people into cults. However, I've also seen prophecy bless people through a timely word that encouraged, strengthened and brought comfort to them. We can't allow fear of abuse to cause us to avoid prophecy and other gifts of the Spirit. In fact, it gives us even more reason to recognize and utilize genuine prophecy in order to equip the saints for their works of service (Ephesians 4:11–13). Mature believers need to carefully weigh prophetic words (1 Corinthians 14:29), and prophecies should always be given in a fitting and orderly way (1 Corinthians 14:40). The bottom line is prophecy should be embraced and exercised today.

1 Corinthians 13:10 refers to when Jesus will one day return. It is my belief and conviction that all the other spiritual gifts listed in 1 Corinthians 12:28, including prophecy, will last among believers until that glorious time when we will see Him face to face. In light of that, there's an even greater timeliness to Paul's instructions in 1 Corinthians 14:1–4 for us to: "walk in the way of love ... and eagerly desire all the spiritual gifts, but especially the gift of prophecy."

11

GOD'S METHOD
OF COMMUNICATING
HIS FRUSTRATION

Tom Lane

⸺⸺⸺

Over the past 100 years, the primary model for prophetic ministry in the Church has been the Old Testament model. The prophet was a person who fell outside the existing leadership of a church and had a different, more "holy" lifestyle. People viewed the prophet as someone appointed and anointed by God as His representative to expose and correct God's wayward saints. The prophet's message was typically delivered with an emotional intensity indicative of God's anger and frustration with an individual or the group as a whole ... usually in a voice full of vibrato, volume and passion that declared God's displeasure with the sinful actions of His people. However, as mentioned earlier in the book, this model of prophetic ministry in the Church is patterned after the prophetic model depicted in the Old Testament and is not at all the model demonstrated in the New Testament. Here are two passages—one from the Old Testament and one from the New Testament—which illustrate the difference between the two models.

❧ Old Testament Model

"Also I have sent to you all My servants the prophets, sending them again and again, saying: 'Turn now every man from his evil way and amend your deeds, and do not go after other gods to worship them. Then you will dwell in the land which I have given to you and to your fore-fathers; but you have not inclined your ear or listened to Me.'"

Jeremiah 35:15 (NASB)

❧ New Testament Model

In the past God spoke to our ancestors through the prophets at many times and in various ways, but in these last days he has spoken to us by his Son, whom he appointed heir of all things, and through whom also he made the universe.

Hebrews 1:1–2 (NIV)

In the Old Testament, God appointed prophets to be His representatives to the people. As His representatives, prophets were given certain responsibilities, including the enforcement of the covenant between God and man. Their ministry often involved the heated denunciation of Israel's sinful behavior and declaration of God's coming punishment for their action. However, the motivation for their words was always God's unquenchable love for His people. The Old Testament is the story of God's covenant with His people. It's the story of their failure to keep their covenant with God, and it's the story of Him calling them from their wayward actions to Himself so they would do their part in fulfilling the covenant:

"When Israel was a child, I loved him, and I called my son out of Egypt. But the more I called to him, the farther he moved from me, offering sacrifices to the images of Baal and burning incense to idols. For my people are determined to desert me. They call me the Most High, but they don't truly honor me."

Hosea 11:1–2, 7 (NLT)

God's frustration with His people always related to their failure to uphold their part of the covenant they had with Him. He expected them to be loyal to Him and for their behavior to reflect that they were His covenant people set apart for Him. And when they didn't, God communicated His heart of frustrated love through the voice and actions of His appointed prophets.

As God's representatives on earth, the prophets were charged with some very specific tasks. It was their assignment to:

- **Enforce Social Justice and Bring about Social Reform**
  The prophets were actively vocal and engaged in calling God's people to social justice and bringing about social reform. In other words, they spoke to the individual actions and behavior of God's people. Amos denounced the rich who afflicted the poor, and he railed against sexual immorality among God's people as well as those who took bribes (Amos 2:6–8; 4:1; 5:11–12; 8:4–6). Hosea spoke against the vices of God's people that were so prevalent in his day including lying, killing, stealing and adultery (Hosea 4:2). He also spoke against idolatry, because God had specifically commanded His people not to have any other gods beside Him (Exodus 20:1). So when idolatry became a part of their behavior, Hosea vehemently denounced it (Hosea 8:5; 11:2) and called people to repentance.

⊛ Proclaim Future Consequences and Impending Judgment for People's Sinful Actions

All of the Old Testament prophets predicted the future, but they didn't do so for the purpose of encouraging speculation or to satisfy curiosity over what the future might hold. They did it to declare God's perspective to His people. In essence, they made sure people knew sin has eternal consequences. Most of the prophetic messages in the Old Testament were originally delivered as public proclamations. They were God's response to the iniquity and apostasy of His people (Jeremiah 11:2-3; Hosea 8:1). It was the prophet's responsibility to proclaim the future consequences for the past sinful behavior of God's people as well as for their continued current violations of the covenant they had with Him. They would also bring a message of encouragement during times of discouragement and brokenness related to God's promise of future deliverance to motivate God's people toward faithful actions. Their prophetic message provided hope for a discouraged people.

⊛ Announce the Coming Messiah and His Eternal Kingdom

Mankind was created for fellowship with God. It was never God's intention for us to spend eternity apart from Him. However, when mankind began to stray from their relationship with God, the prophets were God's voice to call men back to Him:

> *"Return, O backsliding children," says the Lord; "for I am married to you. I will take you, one from a city and two from a family, and I will bring you to Zion."*
> **Jeremiah 3:14 (NKJV)**

The messages of the prophets were a reminder that God had a plan that included them—a message of God's love and care. They were His voice to remind people that in the midst of their painful circumstances and bondage, a Deliverer was coming. And as God's people, they were part of an eternal kingdom with eternal government.

After the last prophetic word in the Old Testament was delivered, there was a silence from heaven that lasted for about 400 years. The silence was finally broken by a forerunner of Jesus who bridged the gap between the old covenant model and the new covenant model. His name was John the Baptist. Matthew 3:1–3 (NKJV) says:

> *In those days John the Baptist came preaching in the wilderness of Judea, and saying, "Repent, for the kingdom of heaven is at hand!" For this is he who was spoken of by the prophet Isaiah, saying: "The voice of one crying in the wilderness: 'Prepare the way of the Lord; make His paths straight.'"*

In John the Baptist's ministry, we can see elements of the Old Testament prophetic ministry, but the angry declaration of God's pending punishment is very much muted. John's ministry is primarily focused on preparing the way for the Lord Jesus Christ. His prophetic voice called people to repentance and focused their hearts and attention on the coming Messiah. Clearly, when you compare the ministry of John to any of the Old Testament prophets, you see something was different; something was changing.

SO WHAT CHANGED?

The old covenant was based on man's performance in relation to God's holy standard, but the angry declaration of God's pending punishment is very much muted. So God instituted a new covenant based on the righteousness of Jesus Christ rather than man's righteous performance in keeping with His law. Under the new covenant, Jesus stepped into man's place to fulfill the requirements of the covenant on man's behalf since we had been unable to fulfill them on our own. And through the new covenant established in Jesus Christ, righteousness was extended to man through grace, not performance. Through Jesus, God's holy demands were met, and the Holy Spirit was given to man so God could once again walk with us in friendship and demonstrate His loving relationship with us.

Hebrews 8:6–13 (NLT) gives us a great explanation of the new covenant and its significance:

> But now Jesus, our High Priest, has been given a ministry that is far superior to the old priesthood, for he is the one who mediates for us a far better covenant with God, based on better promises. If the first covenant had been faultless, there would have been no need for a second covenant to replace it. But when God found fault with the people, he said: "The day is coming, says the Lord, when I will make a new covenant with the people of Israel and Judah. This covenant will not be like the one I made with their ancestors when I took them by the hand and led them out of the land of Egypt. They did not remain faithful to my covenant, so I turned my back on them, says the Lord. But this is the new covenant I will make with the people of Israel on that day, says the Lord: I will put my laws in their minds, and I will write them on their hearts. I will be their God, and they will be my people. And they will not need to teach their neighbors, nor will they need to teach their relatives, saying, 'You should know the Lord.' For everyone, from the least to the greatest, will know me already. And I will forgive their wickedness, and I will never again remember their sins."

When God speaks of a "new" covenant, it means He has made the first one obsolete. It is now out of date and will soon disappear.

Under the new covenant, the voice of God became resident in the hearts of anyone who received Jesus Christ as their Lord through the Holy Spirit.

In His humanity, Jesus was subject to time and space like all human beings. That's why Jesus told His followers it was to their advantage He was leaving them:

> *"Nevertheless I tell you the truth. It is to your advantage that I go away; for if I do not go away, the Helper will not come to you; but if I depart, I will send Him to you."*
>
> **John 16:7 (NKJV)**

In Jesus' absence, the Father sent the Holy Spirit to abide with men and provide help and comfort, to lead them, teach them and bring to their remembrance all He taught them (John 14:26). The responsibilities that had once been given to the prophets—enforcing social justice and bringing about social reform, proclaiming coming judgment for the people's sinful actions and announcing the Messiah and His eternal kingdom was now fulfilled on a personal basis through the Holy Spirit's presence in every believer.

THROUGH JESUS, GOD'S HOLY DEMANDS WERE MET, AND THE HOLY SPIRIT WAS GIVEN TO MAN SO GOD COULD ONCE AGAIN WALK WITH US IN FRIENDSHIP AND DEMONSTRATE HIS LOVING RELATIONSHIP WITH US.

Under the new covenant, the role of the prophet changed from being an enforcer of the covenant to being the impetus behind its application in every believer's life. The purpose of prophetic ministry now is to provide encouragement, comfort and exhortation to the church and individually to God's followers (1 Corinthians 14:3). Fear of embarrassment and humiliation are not part of the equation at all, so we as believers don't have to fear the angry finger of God pointing at us with frustration to correct our misdeeds and failures. We no longer have to fear what God might do or say to expose our failures; instead, we can anticipate the loving affirmation of our heavenly Father. And when we need it, we receive His gentle correction rather than stern rebukes motivated by disappointment and frustration. The new covenant has brought a new expression of prophetic ministry to the individual and the Church. The result is the equipping of the Church and each individual for the work of ministry.

I grew up going to church with my family. Through my parent's leadership and example, we were all actively involved in our church. Through that involvement, I developed a religious knowledge of God. Based on the traditions of the leaders of the church, I learned about Him in a religious way. And based on my efforts to be good, I felt rightly related to Him. However, my relationship was tentative, not personal. I wasn't righteous, and I knew it. No matter how good and diligent my efforts were to please God and be like Him, it was sketchy at best. Some days my performance was better than others, but I didn't have a personal relationship with God until I realized my efforts would never be enough. That's when I acknowledged my need and asked Jesus Christ to be my Savior and Lord. I went from a *religious knowledge* of God to a *personal relationship* with Him!

> **THE NEW COVENANT HAS BROUGHT A NEW EXPRESSION OF PROPHETIC MINISTRY TO THE INDIVIDUAL AND THE CHURCH. THE RESULT IS THE EQUIPPING OF THE CHURCH AND EACH INDIVIDUAL FOR THE WORK OF MINISTRY.**

Now, my interaction with Him through personal relationship is motivated out of love and my heart's desire to be intimately connected to Him—hearing, believing and obeying Him every day. The Holy Spirit's presence guides me and teaches me. Through His work, I feel the love of my heavenly Father in every aspect of my service and involvement with Him. I'm also convicted when my behavior doesn't reflect my love for Him. Whenever my behavior offends God, the Holy Spirit lets me know by convicting me, and I feel the distance in my relationship with Him that sin—my sin—has created. And through the abiding work of the Holy Spirit, I anticipate more than the years I will live on this earth. He helps me anticipate eternity and all the future holds beyond my life on earth.

The Holy Spirit's presence in my life is made possible through my relationship with Jesus Christ. He fulfills every task the Old Testament prophets were once given to fulfill. Their mission is complete and is being fulfilled by another, the Holy Spirit—our Comforter—who is part of the Godhead and who abides with us and in us!

Planning Prophetic Presbyteries

12

PROPHETS, PROPHECY AND PRESBYTERY

Wayne Drain

———

Do not neglect your gift, which was given you
through a prophetic message when the
body of elders laid their hands on you.

1 Timothy 4:14 (NIV)

There are many differing ideas today about what prophets and prophecy are all about. Are they real? Are they spiritual or some sort of demonic hocus pocus magic? Perhaps due to the sheer number of popular books and TV shows that have covered it, many people think they are familiar with the prophetic (although I'm pretty sure TV isn't the best avenue for people to draw conclusions about this powerful ministry). Some lump prophecy in with horoscopes, spiritual readings and fortune-tellers who have late night infomercials, but the source of revelation between these groups is completely different. Sadly though, the majority of Christians today aren't very familiar with the genuine biblical gift of prophecy since many denominations teach that the gifts of the Holy Spirit are not for today. Many only relate to prophecy as it pertains to predicting events of the end times and the return of the Lord Jesus. And while it is certainly an area of interest for many, my focus here is not on end-time prophecy.

Let me say this up front ... I *firmly* believe there are believing men and women of God today who legitimately operate in the gift of prophecy or in the office of the prophet. As they observe the benefits and blessings of prophetic ministry in other congregations, more and more churches are beginning to open the door for God's expression. They are doing what the Apostle Paul encouraged: they "eagerly desire gifts of the Spirit, especially prophecy" (1 Corinthians 14:1, NIV). One way to introduce prophecy to your church body is to host prophetic presbyteries (which we'll explain about in more detail in a later chapter). In my 35-plus years of ministry, I've seen a dramatic increase in interest in prophetic ministry as the number of people who are positively impacted by it increases.

> **THE BIBLE IS CLEAR THAT WE SHOULD ACTIVELY AND CONTINUALLY BE OPERATING IN THE GIFTS OF THE SPIRIT, INCLUDING THE GIFT OF PROPHECY.**

Joel 2:28–29 seems to be taking on an especially timely relevance today as God is pouring out His Spirit on all flesh and many "sons and daughters" are prophesying. At the same time, there is much caution—and rightfully so—among people who move in this dynamic ministry due to extremes (both real and perceived). Paul makes it clear in 1 Corinthians 14:40 that the gifts of the Spirit should function and be expressed in a fitting and orderly way. That being said, the Bible is clear that we should actively and continually be operating in the gifts of the Spirit, including the gift of prophecy. 1 Corinthians 14:3 (NCV) says, "But those who prophesy are speaking to people to give them strength, encouragement, and comfort." As a pastor who moves in prophetic ministry, I have seen this verse come to life numerous times as people I know and serve receive strength, encouragement and comfort through a timely, prophetic word. On the other hand, I've also seen manipulation occur in the name of prophecy. That's why it's so vital for us to develop a biblical understanding of prophets, prophecy and presbytery.

So how do we get started? Where do we begin? As with all the spiritual gifts, we need to first understand the biblical basis for prophetic ministry. Ephesians 4:16 (NIV) says, "From him the whole body, joined and held together by every supporting ligament, grows and builds itself up in love, as each part does its work." In other words, each believer in a local church has a responsibility to do their part because, as the New Living Translation expresses it, "As each part does its own special work, it helps the other parts grow, so that the whole body is healthy and growing and full of love" (Ephesians 4:16). Ever since the church was birthed in the Upper Room on the Day of Pentecost, the Holy Spirit has been pouring out spiritual gifts as He wills. The book of Acts gives us a glimpse into how the early church received and learned to utilize these spiritual gifts for the glory of God. It also gives us glimpses of how these gifts were misused as young believers were growing and maturing in their faith.

Since the early 1970s, I've seen people operating in the different gifts of the Spirit (including the prophetic) in the church where I serve as Senior Pastor in Arkansas. I believe these gifts are specifically intended for the common good of our community rather than simply a new form of entertainment to draw a crowd.

It's important to know prophets and prophecy have been an active part of the life of God's people for thousands of years. The Scriptures show us prophets such as Jeremiah, Isaiah, Ezekiel and Samuel prophesied in the Old Testament, and Simeon and the prophetess Anna prophesied over Jesus in the New Testament (Luke 2). There are many who believe this powerful ministry passed away during the time of the twelve apostles. However, prophecy and the laying on of hands by a presbytery of elders were clearly practiced by the early church:

Do not neglect the spiritual gift within you, which was bestowed on you through prophetic utterance with the laying on of hands by the presbytery.

1 Timothy 4:14 (NASB)

This is why I remind you to fan into flames the spiritual gift God gave you when I laid my hands on you.

2 Timothy 1:6 (NLT)

Several times throughout the New Testament, we see the Holy Spirit speaking to prophets in order to bring direction and guidance. One such instance was when Agabus prophesied to Paul:

Several days later a man named Agabus, who also had the gift of prophecy, arrived from Judea. He came over, took Paul's belt, and bound his own feet and hands with it. Then he said, "The Holy Spirit declares, 'So shall the owner of this belt be bound by the Jewish leaders in Jerusalem and turned over to the Gentiles.'"

Acts 21:10–11 (NLT)

In 1 Timothy 1:18, Paul instructed Timothy—his young son in the faith—to follow the prophecies once made about him, because doing so would help him fight the good fight, hold onto the faith and maintain a good conscience. Timothy had received spiritual gifts through impartation, which was then confirmed through a prophetic word and the laying on of hands of the presbytery. Paul wanted Timothy to make the connection that his calling was a *spiritual* calling. The Bible is consistently clear that whatever has its beginning in the Spirit cannot be completed in the strength of our flesh. Paul knew ministry was challenging, and he wanted Timothy to know where his help would come from.

In his book, *Prophetic Gatherings In The Local Church*, David Blomgren writes:

Soon after these early accounts, the prophetic ministry began to vanish. The church, which once was persecuted, now became popular because of the legalization of Christianity in the fourth century by Constantine. The result was a decline of spiritual power in the church. The gifts and ministries of the Holy Spirit nearly ceased to operate, and the church was plunged into the Dark Ages. The laying on of hands and the presbytery became only a ritual ... Since the time of the Reformation, however, God has been restoring divine principles and truths that were believed and experienced by the early church. At the beginning of the twentieth century, spiritual gifts began to be restored. God has likewise been restoring to the church prophecy and the laying on of hands by the presbytery. It is no longer a mere form nor an empty ritual, but it is again that through which God gives impartation, direction, correction, confirmation and blessing."[1]

I often receive many questions about prophecy like: "How does it work? How do we know it's authentic?" But perhaps the most common question is simply: "What *is* prophecy?" There are a couple of definitions and key terms I've used for quite some time. My favorite definition of prophecy comes from Graham Perrins, a Welsh Bible teacher, who writes, "Prophecy is a living word from a living God to a living people."[2] I love this simple, yet profound explanation of prophecy.

Another definition of prophecy I've found helpful through the years comes from David Blomgren who says, "Prophecy may be defined as a declaration of a message from God not known by natural means but by divine revelation, including prediction as well as anointed proclamation."[3]

There are two distinct types of prophecy that are often confused: *foretelling* and *forth-telling*.

Foretelling is a form of prophecy that is predictive of future events, such as Agabus' prophecy of a coming famine in Acts 11:28. *Forth-telling* or a "telling forth" occurs when a timely word from the Lord is given for edification, exhortation, comfort or warning.

When it comes to prophecy, people usually fall into one of two camps. One camp confines prophecy to what has already been spoken in the Bible. They advocate that prophecy was for another dispensation ... before the canon of Scripture was completed. Another camp sees biblical prophecy as only having to do with end times, such as the eschatological prophecies found in Daniel, 2 Thessalonians and the book of Revelation.

I firmly believe all of the prophecies written down by men under the Holy Spirit's inspiration and leading (and which were eventually canonized into what we call the Bible) are true (2 Peter 1:19–20). It's also true that one day the Lord will return for His Bride. However, I want to specifically focus on the purpose and principles of prophecy available for us to exercise in the here and now.

The Bible speaks of four distinct spheres of prophecy. These four spheres not only continued on after the canon of Scripture was completed, they're also continuing to be expressed today. We took a look at those different spheres in chapter two, and now I want us to look at how prophets, prophecy and prophetic presbyteries function today.

One of the most anticipated gatherings in my church is our annual prophetic presbytery. It is, without a doubt, the best attended and one of the most inspiring events our church does for our congregation. Our presbyteries even attract many from other churches around our area as well as those without a church home. We usually have quite a multi-generational, inter-denominational crowd at one of our typical presbyteries. We never hype it up or do a massive ad campaign. We simply invest in prayer, inform the community and personally invite whomever we can to come out. I realized a long time ago that people aren't looking for another good Power Point presentation or the latest fill-a-pew program; they just want a word from God.

A PRESBYTERY IS A GATHERING SPECIFICALLY SET ASIDE FOR WORSHIP, PRAYER AND PROPHETIC MINISTRY.

So, you may be wondering: "What exactly *is* a presbytery?" A presbytery is a gathering specifically set aside for worship, prayer and prophetic ministry. It usually takes place over a two- to three-day period, in which a prophetic team ministers to individuals who are candidates for leadership and service within as well as outside a local church. In our church, we usually invite three seasoned ministers who have a prophetic anointing and gifting to come to our church and minister in prophecy and impartation.

Here are some terms we use that might help you understand a little bit more about a prophetic presbytery.

- **Presbyter**
  An elder or a mature minister who functions in one or more of the five-fold ministries: Apostles, Prophets, Evangelists, Pastors and Teachers (Ephesians 4:11–13).

- **Presbytery**
  Two or more presbyters working as a team to prophesy prophetic words and impart them through the laying on of hands over leadership candidates the local church has called forth.

- **Candidate**
  Someone the local elders have judged to be a potential leader in some capacity in the church.

When determining who the candidates are, we keep two primary considerations in mind:

1. A candidate should reflect the qualifications of an overseer or deacon pertaining primarily to moral character as mentioned in 1 Timothy 3, such as being faithful to God, family and church. Usually, candidates are already actively serving in some leadership role under the spiritual covering of the local elders.

2. The timing should be right for the season of life that the candidate is in. For example, it may not be ideal timing to consider someone as a candidate if he or she is about to depart for a season of military service.

There are also two different kinds of prophetic words given in a presbytery.

✐ A Word of Direction

This is a word given to help a candidate see the way ahead. Words of direction are found in various places in the Old Testament, such as in 1 Samuel 10:8 when Samuel told Saul to "go down to Gilgal and wait." In 2 Kings 8:1, Elisha told a widow to "go away from this place, for a famine is coming." A New Testament example that has already been mentioned is Agabus' word to Paul in Acts 21:10–11.

I remember one of the early words of direction I received was given by three different people in three different locations from three different nations over a period of three weeks. The prophetic word spoken over me was simply that God was calling me to pastor a church and prophesy to the nations.

I could see a way to do either one of these things, but I struggled quite a bit to discover how to do both at the same time. Everyone told me it had to be one or the other: I could either be an itinerant minister based in a local church but who traveled, or I could be a local pastor. Well, I'm happy to tell you I have pastored the same church for the last 38 years *and* have traveled and ministered in 33 nations!

That word of direction all those years ago helped me face the doubts of well-meaning people even as I wrestled with my own doubts. I took courage from Paul's instructions to Timothy, his son in the faith, to follow after the prophecies once made about him: "So that by following them you may fight the good fight, holding on to faith and a good conscience" (1 Timothy 1:18–19).

⨳ A Word in Season

The second kind of word given in presbyteries is a word in season. Proverbs 15:23 (NKJV) says: "A [timely] word spoken in due season, how good it is!" A word in season could be a word of encouragement at a time when the candidate is discouraged. It might include a phrase or a word only the recipients and the Lord know about. These words not only encourage but also inspire faith for someone to receive the word of the Lord.

How wonderful is it that God would speak about us to someone else! For example, while ministering in a church in Orlando, Florida, I received a word in season for a lady who had been praying the Holy Spirit would speak to her. I later discovered her exact prayer was: "Lord, I ask for a prophetic word from that guy with the funny name (Is Wayne Drain *really* a funny name?!) that I am doing okay." The first words out of my mouth were, "I sense the Lord wants me to tell you that you're doing okay—much better than you think!" Although this wasn't a profound word of direction, the timeliness of it was deeply encouraging to her. It's thrilling to know God really hears our prayers and speaks into our life situations as a good Father would.

Here's a recent letter I received about a timely word in season I gave during a prophetic presbytery in Texas:

Dear Wayne,

I was a pastor for thirteen years prior to becoming an itinerant evangelist/revivalist in 1994. My wife and I have a ministry based in Fort Worth, Texas. For the past five years, we have primarily ministered in Australia and the Pacific islands.

Here's what you said to me on August 21, 2010:

It is right sometimes to take responsibility for some-
thing that wasn't your fault. It's a test of leadership.
The Lord is using a situation to test your leadership.
You are passing the test. You're taking the high road.
That's what Jesus does. September will bring a shift
change. October will bring clarity. By Thanksgiving,
you'll see breakthrough! You'll be able to put 2010 to
bed and embrace 2011 with hope.

I had been involved in a situation for some time, seeking to reconcile friends in ministry who had gone their separate ways. This was vividly brought home because the people involved were all in the presbytery that night and talking for the first time in over a year! There's now been a complete reconciliation in their relationship with each other.

In September, we traveled to Australia where we began a three-month tour of ministry. During our meetings in September, we experienced the greatest hunger and expectation from people we'd ever encountered in all the five years we've been in Australia.

As we continued ministering into October, the Lord began to make clear to me our role in the Body of Christ. We were ministering in a large Baptist church near Brisbane, and at least 500 people responded to an altar call to receive the fullness of the Holy Spirit. It was incredible!

In November, we returned home to Texas to do some ministry there. For years, I had been praying my wife would have a breakthrough in spiritual freedom to express the gifts God has given her. The Sunday before Thanksgiving, she preached for the very first time! She has shared, testified and prophesied many times throughout our 37 years in ministry, but this was the first time she actually preached ... and the Holy Spirit's anointing was all over her!

That very same week, I began to get invitations for the coming year. We already have the fullest calendar we've ever had. I really am able, for the first time in many years, to put this year behind us and enjoy Christmas, knowing that the coming year is already filled with divine connections. Thank you, Wayne, for hearing and sharing.

Larry from Fort Worth

Although I believe anyone can prophesy when a prophetic anointing is present (1 Corinthians 14:31), I've learned that *different people have different measures of gifting.* In my church, we practice these principles in our community groups, our adult and youth groups and our class for new members as well as in our Sunday services. We've discovered, like Philip and the Ethiopian eunuch of Acts 8:26–40, we are increasingly finding prophetic insight helpful in evangelism and mission outreaches. It seems like more and more often evangelists and prophets are teaming up in this strategic hour for the sake of the gospel. We're seeing and hearing credible reports of people operating in the gifts of the Spirit, such as words of knowledge, healing, prophecy and faith. This, in turn, is igniting a fresh passion in believers to share the good news of the kingdom of God. Amazing results are being seen across the world. We are truly living in exciting times!

Paul wrote in 1 Corinthians 14:5 that those who prophesy edify and build up the Church. And that is the primary purpose for prophets, prophecy and presbyteries—to edify and build up the Church. There are so many people and things around us today that tear us down. That's why the prophetic is so necessary.

As a pastor, it's my deep conviction that the ministry taking place during a presbytery is some of the most useful and encouraging ministry we offer our congregation. As our pastoral team follows up with the candidates to discuss and pray about the words given to them, we're always amazed at the profound and lasting impact of this important ministry.

In my church, we also take great care not to neglect the gifts that are imparted when the presbyters lay their hands on us, accompanied by their prayers of impartation and timely words of prophecy. We remember the words given. We talk about them. And we encourage each other to move in the gifts we've been given. Through it all, this pastor has learned that an incredible work can be accomplished in God's kingdom when His people are encouraged, strengthened and comforted.

13

HOW TO STRUCTURE A PRESBYTERY SERVICE

Tom Lane

As we begin this chapter, I want to ask you a couple of questions: "What place does prophetic ministry have in your church? If you're a pastor, do you want the Holy Spirit's work in your church? In your life personally?"

Prophetic ministry should always begin with a desire for the Holy Spirit's work to be expressed in our personal lives, and from there, into the life of the church. It should only be sought as an expression in the church out of a genuine response in our personal lives that's a reflection of our everyday life in the Spirit. Does your church welcome the work of the Holy Spirit? Do you encourage people to pursue God through welcoming the Holy Spirit and His work in all forms? You must do these things in your personal life first.

Teaching a congregation about the Holy Spirit is critical for their spiritual development. And creating an atmosphere for the Holy Spirit's work in people's lives is an essential part of pastoral leadership. If you've had a bad experience with prophetic ministry, I am genuinely sorry. Would you forgive those who caused your hurt and consider what you experienced wasn't God's plan but the imperfect (and hopefully sincere) attempt of men to represent God?

We help people to live in the Spirit by teaching them about the Holy Spirit. (If you need resources to help you, there's a reference guide at the end of this book with a list of study resources.)

PROPHETIC MINISTRY SHOULD ALWAYS BEGIN WITH A DESIRE FOR THE HOLY SPIRIT'S WORK TO BE EXPRESSED IN OUR PERSONAL LIVES, AND FROM THERE, INTO THE LIFE OF THE CHURCH.

We encourage our leaders to welcome, embrace and pursue the Holy Spirit, because He is one of the members of the Godhead and is actively involved in our lives as believers. We're not fearful that teaching and welcoming the Holy Spirit will open the door to weirdness or excess, because we provide oversight to protect against abuse. If something becomes weird or excessive, we're prepared to respond to it with godly wisdom and authority.

Although we want the manifest presence of God in all of our ministry services and various ministries, we don't typically have an emphasis on the expression of the gifts of the Spirit in our weekend worship services. Our focus for those services is worship, the Word and personal ministry. However, our altar ministry team is completely free to operate in the gifts of the Holy Spirit as they minister to people in the service. We also teach and encourage our small group leaders to be open to the Holy Spirit's work in their group meetings and to allow the gifts of the Holy Spirit to be expressed in an orderly fashion.

Once a year, we host a prophetic presbytery in our church where a prophetic team comprised of individuals with the prophetic gifts minister and speak words from God over selected leaders in our congregation. We start the meetings on Sunday night and continue with them on Monday morning, Monday night and Tuesday morning. We allow three or four candidates in each session, so that means we usually have a maximum total of 16 candidates consisting of either couples or singles.

PRESBYTERY MEETING SERVICE STRUCTURE

The elements that make up our presbytery services are worship and a brief teaching about the Holy Spirit, prophecy and prophetic ministry followed by a time of ministry for the candidates by the prophetic team and then prophetic words to individuals in the congregation. We allot approximately 15 minutes of ministry for each candidate (about 45–60 minutes total). Each service is approximately 90 minutes, so we break down our service based on the following time allotments:

- Worship | 15 minutes

- Teaching on the Subject of the Prophetic | 10 minutes

- Prophetic Ministry to the Candidates | 45–60 minutes

- Prophetic Words to the Congregation | 15 minutes

Of course, this service structure is only a guideline and is completely subject to how the oversight pastor leading the service feels it needs to be facilitated based on sensitivity to the Lord's leading in the service. We certainly don't want to over-administrate and hinder the Holy Spirit's work or presence!

PRESBYTERY CANDIDATES

We've held prophetic presbyteries at our church ever since we first began. In the early days, it was easy to identify and select candidates; however, as our church and leadership base have grown, we've implemented a process for selecting leaders to be candidates in the presbytery services from year to year.

After determining the exact number of presbytery candidates, we look at recommendations from our elders, pastors and key ministry leaders for individuals who are emerging leaders, leaders who are transitioning, leaders who have never been through presbytery or those who are new in their ministry service role. We seek to have a blend of vocational ministry candidates and lay ministry leaders. We draw the candidates from the following categories:

- Senior Leadership—Pastoral Team and Elders

- Servant Leadership—Deacons and Ministry Oversight Leaders

- Service Areas—Emerging and Current Leaders from Every Department Area of Ministry

We recognize we have a significant number of single leaders in our congregation, and so we make an effort to look for single candidates in each of the categories. If a candidate is married, we make sure to include their spouse in the presbytery even though only one may be serving in an area of ministry. We recognize that a married couple is a team, and the one who's not involved must still support and be a part of the ministry work of their spouse. Another reason we do this is there are often things revealed that have future ramifications for the couple and their ministry together.

PRESBYTERY CANDIDATE WORDS

During the service, candidates are called forward and seated in the front of the room so the congregation can easily see them and the presbytery team can minister to them. When a candidate or candidate couple is seated, we ask the congregation to join with us as we pray for them and God's ministry to them. After a brief prayer, the presbytery team begins ministering and speaking prophetic words to candidates. When each service concludes, we have a meal available for both the presbyters and the candidates where they can sit and talk through the words that have been given. This preliminary review of the ministry that has just taken place is a great time for information and feedback. During the ministry time, it's common for candidates to not absorb everything that's spoken to them. This post-service meal allows us to have an immediate review, and it's a tremendous encouragement to the candidates as well as the presbyters as they interact over what has just taken place.

REVIEW OF THE CANDIDATE WORDS

As each presbyter speaks to the candidates, the words are recorded during the service. These recordings are later transcribed and a member of our leadership team reviews them with the candidate. We never treat prophetic words as directive; instead, we view them as words of confirmation from a perspective of edification, exhortation and comfort. The review process (which

PROPHETIC PRESBYTERIES ARE SUCH AN EXCITING TIME OF SPIRITUAL REVELATION.

is scheduled with the candidates as quickly as the words can be transcribed—within a month in most cases) helps to identify the application of the word and add confirmation to the words given.

THE PRESBYTERY TEAM

Our senior leadership team selects presbyters whom we know have prophetic gifts and approach prophetic ministry with a similar heart as us. In order for us to select someone as part of a presbytery team, they must have a New Testament mindset for prophetic ministry. Although they don't have to be pastors, they must be a committed and submitted part of a congregation and come with a heart to serve the Lord's purpose for ministry to the candidates.

Once the candidates are determined, a list of their names is given to the presbyters for their prayerful consideration before the prophetic presbytery. This list only contains names; it doesn't include any information that might give the presbyters insight into their ministry function or title. We give the presbytery team the names so, through prayer, the Holy Spirit can begin revealing words to them for the candidates.

There are times when a presbyter may know the candidate. When this is the case, the presbyter will acknowledge they know the candidate but what they share won't be based—to the best of their efforts—on what they may know naturally about the candidate or their circumstances. Our motive, as well as that of the presbytery team in hosting this event, is to see people the way God sees them. Because, ultimately, we know God sees us more deeply and more gifted than we see ourselves. That's why prophetic presbyteries are such an exciting time of spiritual revelation.

Then I fell down at his feet to worship him, but he said to me, "You must not do that! I am a fellow servant with you and your brothers who hold to the testimony of Jesus. Worship God." For the testimony of Jesus is the spirit of prophecy.

Revelation 19:10 (ESV)

14

PROPHECY AND MUSIC

Wayne Drain

While the harpist was playing,
the hand of the Lord came upon Elisha.

2 Kings 3:15 (NIV)

*E*lisha was in a difficult situation. A war was about to break out in Israel. Joram, the new king of Israel, along with the king of Edom and Jehoshaphat, the king of Judah, were about to march out to war against Mesha, the King of Moab. When confusion broke out about which way to attack, Jehoshaphat suggested they find Elisha to see if he might have a word from the Lord for them at this critical moment. When they found the prophet, he made it clear he had little respect for the king of Israel because of the king's sinful ways. But since Elisha *did* respect Jehoshaphat, he said he'd seek the Lord for a word. What Elisha requested next is very insightful:

> *Elisha said, "As surely as the Lord Almighty lives, whom I serve, if I did not have respect for the presence of Jehoshaphat king of Judah, I would not pay any attention to you. But now bring me a harpist."* **While the harpist was playing, the hand of the Lord came on Elisha** *and he said, "This is what the Lord says: I will fill this valley with pools of water."*
>
> **2 Kings 3:14–16 (NLT; emphasis added)**

Elisha understood there is a connection between music and the release of the prophetic. And "as the harpist was playing," Elisha prophesied the word of the Lord.

I was first introduced to this principle years ago. Since then, I have witnessed time and time again how anointed music truly does help to release the prophetic. Many people believe God only speaks today through the words of the Bible. But Job declared: "For God does speak—now one way, now another—though man may not perceive it" (Job 33:14, NIV). The problem isn't that God isn't speaking. The problem is believers have been taught God only speaks through one avenue—the Bible. While the Bible is definitely the primary way God speaks to us, I also believe God speaks in a variety of other ways. And one of the many ways through which God communicates is music.

"God is speaking through the music."[1] Those six words from one of my favorite songs encapsulate the relationship between prophecy and music. When I was a young Christian musician and new pastor, I began to notice many of the leaders in the Old Testament either seemed to be musicians themselves or else they actively partnered with musicians. I didn't understand how music and prophecy worked together, but I was determined to find out. Now, years later, whenever I teach these principles, pastors and musicians often ask me: "I see the connection between music and the prophetic in Scripture too, but how do they practically work together?"

We're continually dealing with the challenge of unbelief, because many people are still not sure whether God actually speaks prophetically today. That's why we must always remember scriptures like Deuteronomy 8:3 (NLT) that remind us: "people do not live by bread alone; rather, we live by every word that comes from the mouth of the Lord." Or there's Jesus' words in John 10:27 (NLT): "My sheep listen to my voice; I know them, and they follow me." The first thing to understand is God is speaking today. And He not only speaks to us today through the prophetic, but also through anointed music.

The word prophecy comes from words that mean "to flow together; to bubble up or gush out a living, prophetic unction that flows out from one's spirit." Prophecy can sometimes be *fore-telling*—announcing future events. But more often, it's *forth-telling*—declaring a "now" prophetic communication from the heart of God relating to a person or situation. I like what Graham Perrins has to say about the connection between music and the prophetic: "When worship and music blend together as an expression of what God is saying and doing in our lives now, it becomes prophetic. It is contemporary and relevant."[2]

While music associated with the church is usually called praise or worship music, we can praise or worship God through all kinds of musical styles and in all kinds of settings—with or without words and with or without instruments. (For example, you can even worship God simply by serving someone at your local Walmart!) The word "praise" comes from words in the Bible that essentially mean to sing *about God*. Miriam, the sister of Moses, sang a song of praise when God parted the Red Sea: "Sing to the Lord, for he has triumphed gloriously; he has hurled both horse and rider into the sea" (Exodus 15:21, NLT). The word "worship" comes from words that mean to turn toward; to kiss; to prostrate oneself; to adore and to heal. Worship happens when we sing or express our worship directly *to God*. The lyrics of a

ANOINTED MUSIC TRULY DOES HELP TO RELEASE THE PROPHETIC.

well-known worship song inspired by one of David's psalms give us a good example of worship: "I love You, Lord. And I lift my voice to worship You. O my soul, rejoice."[3] I often say that prophetic worship happens when worship and a word from God kiss.

It's important to understand the connection between praise, worship, music and prophecy runs throughout the entire Bible. Let me highlight just a few:

- In 1 Samuel 10, we see Samuel's band of prophets and musicians teaming up to communicate God's prophetic message in words, actions and song. They played instruments, danced and prophesied as they moved from place to place.

- The prophet Elisha called for a musician to play, and while he was playing, Elisha prophesied (2 Kings 3:14–16).

- David understood this connection. 1 Chronicles 25 says: "King David and the commanders of the army, set apart some of the sons of Asaph, Heman and Juduthun for the ministry of prophesying, accompanied by harps, lyres, and cymbals."

- Zephaniah 3:17 says, "He will rejoice over us with singing." God Himself sings over us! And when He does, we can't help but respond in faith!

- One of the ways heaven gets involved when we worship God is through "the song of the Lord." Tamara Wilson defines it like this: "The song of the Lord is a song that first belongs to, and then proceeds from the Lord God Almighty."[4] This song often takes place when a discerning musician or singer begins to worship with words, notes or sounds that haven't been previously written, recorded or set down in print. In these special moments, it's not unusual for someone to sing forth a song with a timely word for God's people who have gathered to worship Him.

◈ Ephesians 5:19 encourages God's people to sing "spiritual songs" when we gather together. It makes sense to me that if the Lord surrounds His throne in heaven with worship, then surely it's important for us to give adequate time for praise and worship when we gather.

The first time I remember seeing a musician prophesy through music in our church was on one of the most unlikely instruments—a tuba! When our young church began, we had a large percentage of music majors attending from a local university. One of the music majors who joined our worship team was a young man named Elton. Our worship band consisted of guitars, drums, keyboards, singers and a tuba. Elton was a very good tuba player, but more importantly, he was also spiritually sensitive. I had been teaching about prophesying on instruments as King David had called for in 1 Chronicles 25:1 (NLT):

THE CONNECTION BETWEEN PRAISE, WORSHIP, MUSIC AND PROPHECY RUNS THROUGHOUT THE ENTIRE BIBLE.

"David, together with the commanders of the army, set apart some of the sons of Asaph, Heman and Jeduthun for the ministry of prophesying, accompanied by harps, lyres and cymbals." I was encouraging our little congregation to take some steps of faith and ask the Holy Spirit to use them to do what we had been teaching. The worship band came back to play one last song during our time of altar ministry. As they were playing softly, we began to hear low musical notes resonating off the wooden floor and concrete walls. Elton was playing a melody that wasn't from a song we knew—it wasn't even from a song that Elton knew! He played a beautiful, deep melody that seemed to be coming from heaven. Several of us were aware we were hearing much more than just a few notes coming from a tuba. The Holy Spirit had decided He wanted to sit in and play through the most unlikely instrument in the room. (That's just like Him to do that!)

As Elton was ending his melody, one of the guys in our church stood up and said, "While he was playing that melody, the Lord spoke to me." He then gave a prophetic word full of encouragement that later proved to be an accurate word of direction for our church. Since then, we've seen this play out again and again, through all kinds of different instruments, all kinds of voices and all kinds of people. I've come to firmly believe music and worship can release the prophetic anointing of the Holy Spirit, and I believe prophetic ministry inspires worship. Prophecy and music are a team made in heaven!

During altar calls or prophetic presbyteries, we've seen spiritually sensitive musicians and singers not only prophesy on their instruments but also inspire and release those with gifts of prophecy, words of knowledge and words of wisdom. But how does it work practically?

Here's what seems to work for our congregation. As their senior pastor, I take time to train our musicians, singers, dancers, actors, poets, artists and those with prophetic gifts. I help them understand the divine connection between the creative arts and the prophetic.

But we don't only study these principles from Scripture, we also challenge each other to explore the connection between music and the prophetic in safe environments such as rehearsals, community groups or special monthly services specifically designed for worship and soaking in God's presence. We also expect the Holy Spirit to move among us during our weekend services.

I've heard many music leaders say: "The best spontaneity is well planned." That's why I make sure all of our services have some room to breathe. Here's what I mean by that. Our services can get jam-packed with things we feel have to get done—time-sensitive announcements, baby dedications on the only weekend in-laws can gather, offerings, fundraisers, etc. However, I've found when we don't make room within our service schedule for spontaneity or time to wait on God's leading, we can find ourselves with no room for the Holy Spirit to break in. The Holy Spirit is a gentleman; He'll often wait until we give Him a proper invitation before He begins to move among us with prophetic words or spiritual insight about how to pray or what to focus on in an altar call.

In prophetic-oriented gatherings such as presbyteries, I ask the most spiritually sensitive musicians and singers I have to support the presbyters. Sometimes it only involves one instrument such as a piano or a guitar. Other times, it's a small group consisting of a guitar, bass, drums and keyboard. Our goal is to team up with those who are ministering through the prophetic gifts with anointed music and songs with which the congregation can easily engage and worship. I often ask a piano player or a guitarist to provide gentle, soft instrumental music to help create an atmosphere of faith and receptiveness. As a church, we've been blessed to experience some of the most powerful times of ministry when music and the prophetic flow together in mutually supportive ways. Sometimes during a presbytery, we even hit the pause button on praying and prophesying over the candidates and simply sing a song together. This often seems to re-energize the congregation to lean in and be receptive to this powerful ministry.

But let me emphasize a very important point—the pastor or leader directing the services and the worship leader need to be in sync. The pastor must understand the Holy Spirit just might choose to speak through music to people. Therefore, he or she needs to be supportive and make room for that possibility. One thing that bugs me is when pastors "check out" to review their notes while the congregation worships. It communicates to the worship team and the congregation that worship isn't very important. On the other hand, I completely understand there's a lot of information a pastor has to deal with. I'm often handed notes from well-meaning people reminding me of a significant announcement that didn't get communicated or to be sure and recognize that Sister Bertha turns 80 today! And sometimes, I receive a note or word of encouragement or exhortation that makes me feel like I've found a missing puzzle piece for what the Lord intends for that particular gathering. During worship one

Sunday, I was asking the Lord what sort of appeal I should give at the end of my message. A man handed me a note that said: "I feel the Lord wants to bring people to salvation today." God answered my prayer through that man's note. And sure enough, four people came to salvation on that day! As much as I try to limit distractions during worship, they still come. It's important for leaders in a worship service to remember that people in your congregation who observe you appearing to be disengaged or distracted may conclude worship must not be important to you. And sadly, they may draw the conclusion it doesn't need to be important to them either. Martin Luther once wrote a statement to a friend that I believe with all of my heart: "Next to the word of God, music deserves the highest praise."[5]

The flip side of this coin is the worship leader needs to honor the pastor's direction in terms of time constraints, volume levels and when is the best time to play or not to play. The relationship between the pastor and the worship leader is among the most important relationships in the church. I'm not saying the two have to be best friends, but it *is* important for this relationship to be nurtured outside of regular meetings. They need to be on the same page with each other in order for their partnership to be effective. If the pastor views music as merely an attention-getter or prelude for the message, the church could miss

MUSIC IS A POWERFUL TOOL IN THE HANDS OF ANOINTED MUSICIANS AND SINGERS. COMBINING MUSIC AND THE PROPHETIC— TOGETHER IN UNITY WITH LOCAL PASTORS IS A COMBINATION THAT CAN'T BE BEAT!

something very wonderful. And if the worship leader resists the authority of the leader, the Holy Spirit won't move as freely as He would like to. Unity should be valued and intentionally practiced in our worship services on the weekend as well as throughout the week.

The relationship between Moses and Aaron is a type of pastor/worship leader relationship. The Bible tells us Moses was the leader of the nation of Israel, and his brother Aaron served as the high priest. Moses communicated directly with God. He was even called a friend of God, and the Lord used Moses to deliver His people from the bondage of captivity. God gave the law directly to Moses who then announced it to the children of Israel (Exodus 19–31). In the same way, effective pastors hear from God through prayer and study and then share with their congregations what they've received. Much like worship leaders today, Aaron's primary responsibility was to minister to the Lord and serve Moses (Exodus 7:1–2, 19). The Bible records examples of both when Moses' and Aaron's relationship worked in unity and when it didn't. Moses learned a hard lesson when he rebelled against God's instruction (Numbers 20:1–13). Aaron learned a hard lesson when he chose to rebel against Moses (Numbers 12). I love that the Bible doesn't try to sanitize or gloss over sins and failures to make things appear better. It helps us to see that even super-saints like Moses and Aaron struggled in learning to obey God.

Neither was it always easy for Moses and Aaron to work with other people. Unexpected stuff and difficulties popped up constantly. Disagreements, jealousies and greed cropped up from time to time. We deal with those kinds of complications and issues today as well, and we have an Enemy who is trying to divide and destroy us. That's why Paul's command in Ephesians 4:3 is so important: "Make every effort to keep (maintain) the unity through the bond of peace."

Years after Moses and Aaron died, King David offered insight and wisdom about similar lessons he had learned. David brought a unique perspective to his leadership of Israel as king because he was also a musician and songwriter. He was called the "sweet psalmist of Israel." David understood leadership. He understood worship. He understood the importance of prophecy. And he understood the importance of obeying God's voice and knew it was vital to have honest relationships with God's people. David also realized there is a connection between unity and the release of God's blessings. Look at what he wrote about the power of unity and the precious promise attached to it:

> *How good and pleasant it is when God's people live [dwell, work] together in unity! It is like precious oil poured on the head, running down on the beard, running down on Aaron's beard, down on the collar of his robe. It is as if the dew of Hermon were falling on Mount Zion. For there the Lord bestows his blessing, even life forevermore.*
>
> **Psalm 133:1–3 (NIV)**

Music is a powerful tool in the hands of anointed musicians and singers. It's been said people always remembered more of John Wesley's sermons when his brother Charles put the essence of the message in a song. Prophecy is also a powerful ministry that can have a huge impact on those who receive it. Combining these two ministries—music and the prophetic—together in unity with local pastors is a combination that can't be beat!

What we do at my church may not work for you in exactly the same way. So I encourage you to seek the Lord about the most effective way you can bless your congregation with the powerful ministry of music and prophecy. I've seen the Holy Spirit accomplish more in people's lives during five minutes of anointed music that releases the prophetic than I've seen in a year of pastoral counseling. I can honestly testify God is speaking through the music. I encourage you to open up the doors and let the music play. You'll be glad you did!

Making Room
for
Prophetic Ministry
in Your Church

15

MANAGING AND DEVELOPING THE PROPHETIC

Tom Lane

───────

Easter was quickly approaching, and we were busy making plans to combine our four weekend services into one service at an off-site location that just happened to be the civic auditorium of our city. I was told by some of our leaders that a couple—who had once been a part of the church but had left offended—was planning to come and deliver a prophetic word in our Easter service. I contacted the couple to verify their plans and asked them to come in and discuss their "word" before they came to the service. After reluctantly agreeing to come in, they told me they were accountable to God, and if we wouldn't receive their "word," the Lord would remove His presence from the church and inflict the full force of His judgment. We politely told them we didn't receive their "word" as being from God, and if they attempted to disrupt the service, security would usher them out. They ended up coming to the Easter service and sitting on the front row, but they held their word to themselves.

When prophetic ministry is viewed as the expression of God's work to expose sin, call rebellious people and leaders back to His service and generally oppose imperfect leadership with no accountability whatsoever for the prophet except for God, is it any wonder that it's often unwelcome and resisted by those responsible to care for and lead the church? Ministry like this is terrifying for any pastor and church who desire to know and experience the presence of God and serve Him in ministry to people. After all, what pastor in his right mind would reject a word from God

WE NEED TO TEACH, TRAIN AND DEVELOP A NEW GENERATION OF PROPHETS FOLLOWING THE NEW TESTAMENT MODEL OF PROPHETIC EXPRESSION.

at the risk of bringing God's judgment on the church? So, in our desire to err on "God's" side, we many times ignore what we instinctively feel and allow a person with an offense against the leadership to impose their word of terror on the church body. Some mistakenly think the prophetic is God's method for bringing correction to leadership and insuring they walk in humility before Him. As a result, they try and place their belief on others through guilt and intimidation.

When the church operates under this Old Testament understanding of the prophetic, certain dynamics are created that make managing and developing the prophetic difficult. Experiences like the one I dealt with that Easter can cause pastoral leadership to establish a defensive perimeter around the congregation to keep people with an offense at bay. It takes just one or two of these kinds of experiences for the leadership of the church to take a protective position designed to keep a few independent wounded people from taking out their frustrations on the congregation and its leaders. Their aggressive and misguided prophetic expression damages people in the name of God and destroys God's work using His name as justification for the destructive results. In contrast, the New Testament model of prophetic ministry was both connected to the Church and used as a powerful tool to encourage and build up the entire congregation as well as individual believers.

We need to teach, train and develop a new generation of prophets following the New Testament model of prophetic expression. Using the numerous stories recorded throughout the book of Acts as our foundation, we need to raise up servants who are part of the congregation of believers to use their God-bestowed gifts to build and strengthen the church. We find one such account in Acts 13:1–3 (NIV, emphasis added):

> *Now in the church at Antioch* there were prophets and teachers*: Barnabas, Simeon called Niger, Lucius of Cyrene, Manaen (who had been brought up with Herod the tetrarch) and Saul. **While they were worshiping the Lord and fasting, the Holy Spirit said,** "Set apart for me Barnabas and Saul for the work to which I have called them." So after they had fasted and prayed, they placed their hands on them and sent them off.*

Those three short verses tell us several important things. First, there were prophets and teachers recognized within the church. Their ministry didn't function outside the church; instead, they were in relationship and accountable to their fellow believers in the church. If they got weird, religious or überspiritual, they were accountable due to their relationships within the church which brought balance and correction. The relationships brought balance and correction to them as it does to all who are relationally related in ministry. The same thing applied if their ministry wasn't fruitful and caused damage to the body of believers. The implication is clear that the service of these prophets and teachers was to God in the context of their relationship to the church leadership and each other. It seems fairly obvious their commitment and submission to God's work and leading was guided by their relationships in the church. Second, prophetic ministry was recognized, validated and received in the church as a ministry beneficial to the entire body of believers. Under this healthy relational dynamic, prophetic expression was embraced rather than rejected. It was accepted, encouraged and valued rather than resisted. Third, prophetic ministry was a catalyst for recognizing and sending people into their ministry assignments. While it wasn't the only method God used to speak and direct believers toward identifying and walking in their specific ministry and assignment, it was definitely a clear and confirming voice to those in the church as well as the leaders of the church related to God's anointing, direction and selection of individuals for specific ministry roles.

LEGITIMIZING PROPHECY

Does God speak today? And if He does, then what methods does He use to speak? Is it appropriate to use a scriptural lens to evaluate what's being said when God speaks, or should I accept without question what's given as from God? If prophecy is one of the ways God speaks, then where and how should it be expressed?

For every person who's submitted to pastoral leadership, these questions must be answered so prophetic ministry can be developed in a proper way. If God says something to a person in our congregation, how do they know if they're supposed to share it, when they're supposed to share it and how they're supposed to share it?

In addition, simply being open to what God may want to do through the prophetic doesn't automatically legitimize its expression. Developing and managing prophetic ministry in your church must first begin by giving it a legitimate place. And if you want to give expression to the prophetic in your church, then a biblical foundation must be laid through preaching and teaching.

A local church can't be ruled by feelings or personal opinions. Defined boundaries for and methods of prophetic expression must be identified. A structure needs to be established for developing, managing and monitoring people's expression of the prophetic, because without proper leadership, anything—not just the prophetic—has the potential of becoming weird. The church is God's place of corporate work and expression and, as such, must be a reflection of Him. *All* ministry must be founded on biblical principles and reflect the nature and character of God. Prophecy is a spiritual gift that results from the Holy Spirit's work *through* an individual *to* another individual or group, and recognizing that must be based on a biblical foundation with a clear respect for God-appointed authority.

Developing a strategic plan for prophetic ministry is a necessary part of legitimizing it for your church. Healthy things grow in developmental stages. So when you legitimize the prophetic and its expression in your church, you can feel comfortable to allow it to grow according to a plan rather than feeling pressure to authorize every form of prophetic expression all at once.

DEFINING PROPHETIC BOUNDARIES

Once prophecy is given a legitimate place in your church, it needs leadership. Someone needs to be identified to lead and oversee the development of prophetic ministry as well as people with prophetic gifts in the church. Ultimately, every ministry of the church is subject to the governing leadership of the church, so the person appointed to lead and oversee prophetic ministry is responsible to reflect the heart and values of the governing authority of the church. If your church is new to prophetic ministry, then the first responsibility of the person appointed to lead and oversee is to make sure the senior pastor, elders or trustees are in full agreement with the direction and boundaries being established. It should be obvious from what I'm saying that you shouldn't encourage or

ALL MINISTRY MUST BE FOUNDED ON BIBLICAL PRINCIPLES AND REFLECT THE NATURE AND CHARACTER OF GOD.

attempt prophetic expression in your worship services without the full support of your senior pastor and governing leadership. If there has been a previous openness to prophetic ministry in your church but its expression has either been out of order or it reflected an Old Testament model, then redirection and training will be necessary as you identify and apply new boundaries for the expression of prophetic ministry.

As you instruct your congregation on the biblical parameters for expressing spiritual gifts—and specifically prophecy—be sure to include biblical guidelines in addition to the unique guidelines established by your church's leadership. Here are a few to consider:

1. If there is public prophetic expression, there will be public evaluation of the word and, if necessary, public correction of the word and the individual delivering the word.

2. Any word that's given must reflect a heart of surrender to God and His appointed leaders in the church. Without that recognition, the word would come from a heart of rebellion, and God doesn't minister from rebellion.

3. Any prophetic word will be judged by the Scriptures and must represent the nature and spirit of God and His Word. If the word is given in a harsh, demeaning or condescending manner, it will be judged as not from God. The Bible tells us prophetic ministry is for building up individuals and the body of believers, and it is to be edifying, encouraging and comforting (1 Corinthians 14:3).

4. Any prophetic expression must be given at an appropriate time in a service or meeting. If it disrupts the flow and isn't submitted to the leadership of the meeting or service,

the word will be judged as inappropriate, regardless of the content. Scripture tells us the spirit of the prophet is subject to the prophet, so the timely expression of a word is under an individual's control and determination.

5. Prophetic ministry confirms, edifies, comforts and exhorts. It doesn't direct, manipulate or require action from the individual in response to the person delivering the prophetic word. If the individual receiving the word isn't moved by God to make the word a part of their life, then no action on their behalf is required or expected.

DEVELOPING PROPHETIC TEAMS

Once the governing authority of the church has legitimized prophetic ministry and boundaries have been identified, the next step is to train and develop teams for prophetic ministry. You can begin your recruitment process by communicating to the congregation when and where prophetic ministry training will take place. By communicating this, you'll draw individuals who are not only interested in being trained but who may also have already sensed a prophetic gift from the Holy Spirit.

Begin your prophetic training with biblical instruction regarding the prophetic as the foundation for each team member. The book of 1 Corinthians clearly differentiates between prophetic ministry and a prophetic word given to an individual by the Holy Spirit's leading. *Any* person can be used by the Holy Spirit to bring a word of encouragement, exhortation or comfort that can benefit an individual or the congregation (1 Corinthians 14:3).

WHILE PROPHETIC MINISTRY SHOULD BE EXPRESSED INSIDE THE CHURCH, IT ALSO NEEDS TO BE EXPORTED OUTSIDE THE CHURCH.

But when an individual is given the gift to deliver these words with regularity and is recognized by the church leadership, he or she has a prophetic ministry.

Your training also needs to clearly communicate what the boundaries are for prophetic expression and ministry. Let people know what mechanisms and relational processes you have in place to enforce the boundaries if they aren't followed. Make it clear that, although the words are believed to come from God, those who minister the words must be submitted to church leadership, and accountability is required in order for teams and individuals to develop their gift and serve in an effective and orderly way.

After you've given biblical instruction and your boundaries are clear, the final step is to create opportunities for ministry. The reason for all ministries in the church is two-fold: 1) to help people; 2) to train and prepare people to represent God outside the church. As we train people for prophetic ministry, we need to instruct them on the best way to deliver their message so even those who aren't familiar with church can receive God's work.

Finally, while prophetic ministry should certainly be expressed *inside* the church, it also needs to be exported *outside* the church. Not everyone knows God speaks today or even expects He would speak to the needs of their particular situation. But even though people may not be aware, it doesn't change the reality that everyone needs to hear from God, because *one word from* God changes *everything* in our lives.

TYPES OF PROPHETIC EXPRESSION

The governing oversight of the church in conjunction with the pastoral leadership should decide how the gifts of the Holy Spirit are expressed in their church. Contrary to what some might feel, managing the time, place and method of prophetic expression within a worship service doesn't quench the Holy Spirit or stifle His expression any more than establishing a timeline for worship and preaching with predetermined time parameters limits God's ability to work through those ministry expressions in a service. Managing the expression of the prophetic gives it a legitimate place and method of expression. In addition, while the traditional method of prophetic expression for many churches is within the context of the worship service, that's not the only place gifts of the Spirit can be manifested. Once prophetic ministry is embraced, it's important to identify opportunities for ministry expression other than during worship in the service. Here are some other places where prophetic expression has been a blessing in our congregation.

1. **In Small Groups**
   The small group ministry of the church is an important place for relational connection and discipleship. The expression of the gifts of the Holy Spirit and specifically prophecy can be especially beneficial in a small group. Having a smaller context makes it easier to know the person who gives the prophecy, and if the prophetic word needs to be corrected, it can be easily done with a limited amount of embarrassment to the person giving the prophetic word. However, if this ministry *is* going to be encouraged in small groups, then leaders must be trained in the doctrine and practice of properly facilitating the spiritual gifts.

2. **With New Members**
   If your process for involvement and service in your church incorporates a new members class, it can be a useful tool of encouragement to have a prophetic team give words and speak over those entering into membership and service at the church. Depending on the size of your new members class, it can be done with teams at the end of the class or it can be done on a special night or series of nights where teams are assigned to rooms in the building and new members are assigned to a time and a room for their prophetic ministry time. When doing this, we recommend for the words to be recorded and an audio recording be given to each new member after the night of ministry (either that night itself or at a later time when the tech team has had time to copy the recording and make it available).

3. **Altar Ministry**

Once prophetic teams have been identified and trained, they can be incorporated into your altar ministry teams that pray for those who respond to ministry during or after a service. Because the individuals will have already been trained, they will understand the foundation and boundaries for their ministry expression to people. And if members of the team are properly identified by wearing a badge or being in a specific location, then people who want or need a word of encouragement, edification or comfort can easily go to a team member for ministry.

4. **Prophetic Presbytery**

Once or twice a year, a time can be set aside to identify leaders or emerging leaders for prophetic presbytery. Ask individuals who are recognized as having the gift of prophecy to come in and minister to your candidates. You can then record and later transcribe the words given to review with each candidate for accuracy and application to their life and ministry.

5. **Words in Season in a Ministry Service**

This is a special event or a time in a service when a prophetic team delivers prophetic words to individuals who are called out of the congregation. When this takes place, the pastoral leadership should guide and confirm the ministry to individuals as they provide oversight and leadership for the ministry service.

6. **Additional Ways to Include the Prophetic into the Life of Your Church**

Here are some additional ways we are developing prophetic ministry at Gateway. You might use these as a catalyst for developing your own expression of the prophetic. These certainly don't all need to be initiated at once, but you can use them one at a time to gradually build the vision and structure for the ministry.

a. A Prophetic Track in Your Discipleship or Sunday School Program
Offer one class per semester with a prophetic theme (prophetic prayer, prophetic worship, prophetic evangelism, etc.).

b. Prophetic Training Class
Offer training classes one night a week for four–five weeks. Make this session available several times a year.

c. Prophetic Leadership Events
Once a year, minister prophetically to a group of leaders in your church or associated with your church. Select candidates and include worship, a short explanation of prophetic ministry and breakouts.

d. Themed Prophetic Events
Hold a special time of prophetic ministry for graduating seniors, small group leaders, single leaders, women's and men's ministry small groups or any other specific group within your church.

e. Conference Breakouts for Prophetic Ministry
Schedule a time and place within a conference for individual and group prophetic ministry.

f. Global Ministry Prophetic Teams
Empower a small team to minister prophetically to church leaders who visit from other nations.

g. Webpage
On your church website, include a section with dates and times of upcoming prophetic events and information on how to get involved.

Many homes have a fireplace that provides warmth, comfort and a place for the family to gather. The fireplace is built with a firebox that contains the fire, channels the smoke through the roof and directs the heat from the fire to be enjoyed. Without the firebox, the fire would be uncontained, and it would become destructive ... possibly to the point of burning down the house. The Holy Spirit and His gifts are like a fire in the heart of God's people. Although we certainly don't manage Him, we can manage and develop a place for His work within the Church body. The guidelines we've discussed in this chapter function like a firebox to contain and direct the work of the Holy Spirit so the fruit of His work and presence in us and our congregations is love, joy, peace, patience, kindness, gentleness, goodness and self-control to His praise and glory!

16

PROPHECY AND THE
DEDICATION OF CHILDREN
Wayne Drain

---

*"So now I give him to the Lord. For his whole life
he will be given over to the Lord."*

1 Samuel 1:28 (NIV)

One of my favorite privileges as a pastor is getting to be involved in the dedication of children. I always enjoy this sweet and tender time with the family, and it's such a blessing to get to connect in this way with members of my church.

In our church, we don't practice infant baptism, because we don't see a clear Scriptural basis for it. Instead, we practice "believer's baptism" as defined by Mark 16:16 (NIV): "Whoever believes and is baptized will be saved, but whoever does not believe will be condemned." This means we baptize those who are old enough to understand the commitment they're making when they receive Christ as their Savior and Lord. We do, however, see a strong Scriptural basis for the dedication of children.

The book of 1 Samuel tells the story of Hannah, a woman who had not only been barren, but also suffered ridicule from other women because of her condition. Desperate to have a child, Hannah vowed: "Lord Almighty, if you will only look on your servant's misery and remember me, and not forget your servant but give her a son, then I will give him to the Lord for all the days of his life" (1 Samuel 1:11, NIV).

When Eli the priest observed Hannah's anguished and grief-filled prayers, he said to her, "Go in peace, and may the God of Israel grant you what you have asked of him" (1 Samuel 1:17, NIV).

1 Samuel 1:20 (NIV) says simply: "So in the course of time Hannah became pregnant and gave birth to a son. She named him Samuel, saying, 'Because I asked the Lord for him.'" And true to her vow, Hannah went back to Eli after weaning little Samuel and reminded Eli of his word for her: "I prayed for this child, and the Lord has granted me what I asked of him. So now I give him to the Lord. For his whole life he will be given over to the Lord" (1 Samuel 1:27–28, NIV). Then Hannah prayed a beautiful prayer of thanksgiving and praise as she dedicated her son Samuel to the Lord:

> *"My heart rejoices in the Lord; in the Lord my horn is lifted high. My mouth boasts over my enemies, for I delight in your deliverance. There is no one holy like the Lord; there is no one besides you; there is no Rock like our God. Do not keep talking so proudly or let your mouth speak such arrogance, for the Lord is a God who knows, and by him deeds are weighed. The bows of the warriors are broken, but those who stumbled are armed with strength. Those who were full hire themselves out for food, but those who were hungry are hungry no more. She who was barren has borne seven children, but she who has had many sons pines away. The Lord brings death and makes alive; he brings down to the grave and raises up. The Lord sends poverty and wealth; he humbles and he exalts. He raises the poor from the dust and lifts the needy from the ash heap; he seats them with princes and has them inherit a throne of*

honor. For the foundations of the earth are the Lord's; on them he has set the world. He will guard the feet of his faithful servants, but the wicked will be silenced in the place of darkness. It is not by strength that one prevails; those who oppose the Lord will be broken. The Most High will thunder from heaven; the Lord will judge the ends of the earth. He will give strength to his king and exalt the horn of his anointed."

1 Samuel 2:1–10 (NIV)

After her prayer, Hannah gave Samuel to Eli to train up in the service of the Lord. 1 Samuel 2:11 (NIV) tells us: "The boy ministered before the Lord under Eli the priest." Little Samuel went on to become a mighty prophet of God, used in powerful ways in the time of King Saul and King David.

There are also various other accounts in the Bible of children being dedicated to God. My favorite is found in Luke 2 where we read the story of Mary and Joseph going up to Jerusalem to consecrate Jesus to God. This passage tells us a devout man named Simeon had heard the Holy Spirit tell him he wouldn't die before seeing the long-awaited promised Messiah:

Now there was a man in Jerusalem called Simeon, who was righteous and devout. He was waiting for the consolation of Israel, and the Holy Spirit was on him. It had been revealed to him by the Holy Spirit that he would not die before he had seen the Lord's Messiah. Moved by the Spirit, he went into the temple courts. When the parents brought in the child Jesus to do for him what the custom of the Law required, Simeon took him in his arms and praised God, saying: "Sovereign Lord, as you have promised, you may now dismiss your servant in peace. For my eyes have seen your salvation, which you have prepared in the sight of all nations: a light for revelation to the Gentiles, and the glory of your people Israel." The child's father and mother marveled at what was said about him. Then Simeon blessed them and said to Mary, his mother: "This child is destined to cause the falling and rising of many in Israel, and to be a sign that will be spoken against, so that the thoughts of many hearts will be revealed. And a sword will pierce your own soul too."

Luke 2:25–35 (NIV)

Simeon wasn't the only prophet in the temple that day. Luke 2 goes on to say:

There was also a prophet, Anna, the daughter of Penuel, of the tribe of Asher. She was very old; she had lived with her husband seven years after her marriage, and then was a widow until she was eighty-four. She never left the temple but worshiped night and day, fasting and praying. Coming up to them at that very moment, she gave thanks to God and spoke about the child to all who were looking forward to the redemption of Jerusalem. When Joseph and Mary had done everything required by the Law of the Lord, they returned to Galilee to their own town of Nazareth. And the child grew and became strong; he was filled with wisdom, and the grace of God was on him.

Luke 2:36–40 (NIV)

These two accounts of the dedications of Samuel and Jesus inspired me years ago to consider the thought that perhaps there should be more to a baby dedication than just dressing a baby up and gathering the family to hear prayers and take pictures. While these things are fine, enjoyable and capture the moment in our memories, adding an element of prophetic ministry not only blesses the children but can actually offer words of exhortation, encouragement and comfort (1 Corinthians 14:3).

Ben is a young man in our church I had the privilege of dedicating 16 years ago. Here's a testimony from Ben's dad about that experience:

In October of 1997, my wife, Jennifer, and I had our son Ben dedicated. During the dedication, Wayne shared that the Lord had given him a word for Ben. Wayne prophesied Ben would be "busy and most happy when creating." Wayne went on to say: "I hear music in his life. I see characters he brings to life." Wayne then continued to describe Ben's relationship with and feelings for his church: "Ben will be a true son of this house. He will love the church in time."

Ben is now sixteen years old and spends much of his spare time either rehearsing with his band, attending play production rehearsals, competing in forensics tournaments or sitting with his guitar singing and writing songs. Today, we are incredibly blessed as parents to hear him often talk with affection about how precious church is to him and describe church as his family.

But there was another particularly significant portion of the prophetic word given in Ben's dedication describing a unique ministry that would develop in his life: "He will work on the edges of the church ... out on the fringes of the church where the hurting people are. He will be a bridge to those coming out of darkness into the light. Mom and Dad, don't be overly alarmed when he hangs out with others of questionable character. His character will answer their questions. Stay close to him, but give him room to explore his field of service."

Ben's musical and dramatic pursuits have often taken him to the fringes of the church into places where creative, intelligent and broken teenagers are. One of these teenagers is Chris. Through a few shared classes and mutual participation in play productions, Ben and Chris became friends. Chris, who is extremely witty and outspoken, publically described himself an atheist and didn't hesitate to poke fun at religion. Ben, however, saw great value in Chris and refused to be satisfied to let his friend remain without God. Jennifer and I found ways to support and guide Ben in his relationship with Chris. We read through the transcript of Ben's dedication again, discussed it with him and began praying for whatever God wanted to do in Chris through Ben.

Chris gradually began attending youth meetings with Ben, then spending the night at our house routinely on Saturday nights to attend services with us on Sunday mornings. Ben made a conscious effort to prioritize his relationship with Chris, turning down opportunities, including a summer internship program that would require him to be away from home all summer. Eventually, Chris decided to attend a youth camp with our youth group. At the Monday night service, I watched with tears in my eyes as Chris stepped into the aisle, responding to a call for salvation to give his heart to Jesus. As Ben stood there, raising his hands toward God, Chris' empty seat beside him, I remembered all the ways over the past year or two Ben had extended himself in love to Chris. I heard the Lord say in that moment: *You know, there's no greater love than to lay your life down for your friends.*

And though Chris is perhaps the most personal example to me, he isn't the only example of how the prophetic word spoken over Ben at his baby dedication is being fulfilled in his life. I couldn't count the number of teenagers of "questionable character" he has brought home after a show or on the weekend. I often hear him in our living room engaging in dialogue, encouraging others who question God's existence or love for them. Ben's prophetic word at his baby dedication has served to affirm him of God's unique call on his life. In addition, it has comforted and reassured us, as his parents, as we buy pizza, watch our refrigerator being routinely raided by hungry teenagers and listen in as Ben's character answers their questions.

That God would speak to us about our children is a wonderfully terrifying thing—but it is so well worth it. I've often personally wondered if I might have avoided some wasted years in my youth had I received this wonderful ministry over my life. And as a pastor, I've been incorporating prophetic ministry when we have baby dedications long enough now to see the incredible benefit and hear the testimonies of young men and women making clear connections with the prophetic words spoken over them at their dedication.

Perhaps you're wondering how to practically involve prophetic ministry as part of children's dedications in your church or family. Before describing how we do things in our church, let me encourage you to seek God to discover what works best for you. When I'm asked to dedicate someone's child, the parents and I determine together the best time family members can gather within the next few weeks in one of our weekend services. (Some family members travel great distances to be there for this important family gathering.) I ask for the name of the child to be dedicated and a picture of him or her I can keep until the dedication. Then, I set aside time to look at the picture and pray for the child and the family. I ask the Lord to reveal to me anything I should pray and prophesy over the child. Finally, I type or write down what I hear. Our office staff then prepares a dedication certificate for the parents to have, and I include a typed version of the word I receive that can be suitable for framing. Many parents have put these words up in their children's rooms for them to see as they grow up.

On the day of their dedication, usually during a time of worship, I call the family and child up in front of the congregation and do five things:

- I encourage the family to dedicate themselves to bringing up their child in the fear and admonition of the Lord.

- I challenge us, as a congregation, to dedicate ourselves to supporting the parents and child as their church family.

- I speak over the child from the prophetic word I received.

- I pray a prayer of blessing over the child and family.

- We make an audio recording for parents to keep and refer to through the years. (Many parents ask a friend to videotape the dedication as well.)

I encourage leaders who are involved in this wonderful ministry to children and their families to note some important elements of prophetic dedication. I've often wondered if there might be a time the Lord would refuse to give me a word for a child. But so far, it seems as if the Lord delights in this ministry as much as I do. Sometimes I sense the Lord is just waiting for me to ask Him for a word to bless the little ones. As you see in Ben's testimony, these words are taken seriously and can be a tremendous encouragement to the children and their families all throughout their lives.

If you're a leader in your church involved in dedications, you'll have to be personally invested. Church leaders, especially pastors, have extremely busy schedules. Because of this, many leaders succumb to the temptation to repeat the same things over and over. It's easier. It seems the fair thing to do so as not to appear to prefer one family more than others. The reasons go on and on. And today, there's an increased availability of sermons online. With many recorded and written accounts of services so readily available, it's easy to find prayers or words spoken over others during dedication services. If you're tempted to use these, don't! Prophetic ministry takes time in preparation. Prophetic words must never be borrowed from others or made up just to please people.

If you choose to include a prophetic element into the dedication, you'll need to prophesy what you personally hear from God. Each child is unique. Each child has his and her own God-given destiny. If you don't move in a prophetic gift yourself, determine if there are those in your congregation who do that you trust. Ask them to co-labor with you. It is well worth the effort.

Raising children is a monumental task. I believe there are countless young Samuels and Bens in your church whose parents are crying out to God for direction and encouragement. Prophetic words spoken over a child can bring much needed encouragement, edification, comfort and direction for the child and the entire family.

17

PROPHECY AND AFFIRMATION OF NEW MEMBERS

Wayne Drain

---

*Therefore, from now on, we regard
no one according to the flesh.*

2 Corinthians 5:16 (NKJV)

$\mathcal{E}$arly in my ministry, I felt the Holy Spirit prompt me to try and see people as God sees them rather than how they may view themselves. As humans, we often see ourselves as being less important and having less value than how God sees us. The truth is God loves and values people so much He sent His only Son to die for us in order that we might become His sons and daughters. God views us as "the glorious ones in whom is all His delight" (Psalm 16:3, NIV). And at the church I pastor, our congregation values getting to know who people are according to the Spirit as much as they do getting to know what people do in the natural.

To illustrate what I mean by that, I want to share with you the story of a man who joined our church several years ago. This man (whom I'll call Bill) signed up for our four-week new members class called *Check It Out*. In this class, we cover our history, vision, core values and the nuts and bolts of how we do life together as "the Church." We hope to give potential members enough information to make an informed and Spirit-led decision about making a commitment to join the church. During the first session of the class, we usually ask for relevant information such as the individual's contact numbers, family, interests and areas where they've served before, but I never personally look at that information until after the fourth and final session of our class.

At the beginning of this particular class, Bill wrote down he had driven a bus for the church he belonged to before his job transferred him to our town. Although driving a bus is an honorable and important area of service, Bill simply viewed himself as only someone who served as a bus driver to pick up those who needed a ride to church meetings. God saw something more for Bill.

The last session of *Check It Out* is what we call an Affirmation Class, because we recognize an essential element of any healthy relationship is affirmation of each other. Affirmation is simply "the act of affirming," which the dictionary defines as "to declare or state positively, to confirm or ratify, to make firm." The purpose of this session is to affirm those joining our church with a time set aside for our elders and those with recognized prophetic gifts to pray and prophesy over each new member. Time and time again, people tell me the Affirmation Class is a key element that helped confirm they had made a good choice to make our church their home.

When it was time to pray over Bill in our Affirmation Class, I prophesied over him he would do the work of an evangelist and he and his wife would walk in other nations ministering the gospel of the kingdom. At the time, Bill wasn't married, but he told me he had been praying for a wife. He also told me he had served as a bus driver in his previous church because no one else had volunteered. He further revealed he had long dreamed of having the privilege of traveling to far-off places and preaching the gospel.

After that day, Bill took active steps of faith to learn about the gospel and sharing his faith. He quickly grew into his calling as a powerful evangelist who won many people to Christ. A few years later, Bill married, and he and his wife began traveling to other nations sharing the good news of Jesus. I'm so glad we didn't assume because Bill had experience as a bus driver, he should serve in the same capacity in our church!

So how do prophecy and affirmation work together? While they may not work together in the exact same way in other churches as they do in mine, I see no reason why the idea of combining the two shouldn't be considered and explored. I have witnessed firsthand its tremendous value in the lives of people who have benefited from this ministry.

Let me explain how we incorporate prophecy and affirmation together in our church. Our *Check It Out* class is usually made up of four sessions as follows:

- Week #1 | History and Vision Class

- Week #2 | Core Values Class

- Week #3 | Nuts and Bolts of Church Life Class

- Week #4 | Affirmation Class

In our Nuts and Bolts of Church Life Class, we explain what the Affirmation Class is about and how it works, because for many, it's something they've never experienced before. During the Affirmation Class, one of our leaders takes a few minutes to explain what biblical prophecy is and how it works. We usually sing a worship song or two and ask the Lord to help us "see" as "He sees." Then we ask each new candidate for membership to come forward. Our team of elders and those with prophetic gifts pray for and prophesy over each new member in turn as the Lord leads. This is usually a very gentle and encouraging time. In conclusion, our elders lay their hands on the candidates as we pray a prayer of confirmation and welcome them as new members. During the following weekend service, we publicly recognize and welcome those who've just completed *Check It Out* as members of our congregation. It's an incredibly encouraging event for everyone involved.

Here are some guidelines we use to administrate our Affirmation Class:

Pre-Affirmation Class Preparation

1. Explain what the Affirmation Class is about in the Nuts and Bolts of Church Life Class. (Be sure to welcome questions for clarification.)

2. Set aside a time for the Affirmation Class and emphasize its importance to the new member candidates.

3. Invite a ministry team of appropriate leaders and those with proven prophetic gifts.

4. Call or email everyone as a reminder a few days before the class.

5. Send the names of the new member candidates to the ministry team and encourage them to confirm their participation and spend time in prayer for the potential new members.

6. Plan for your audio technicians to have the class recorded.

ø Order of Affirmation Class

1. The *Check It Out* pastor welcomes everyone and gives a brief explanation of the biblical gift of prophecy.

2. A musician leads a brief time of worship (one or two songs).

3. One of our leaders prays for the Holy Spirit to anoint us as we pray and prophesy.

4. The *Check It Out* pastor calls for each individual candidate or married couple to come to the front to be prayed for.

5. Usually two to four leaders offer prayers or words of prophecy.

6. One of our elders offers a prayer to receive the candidates as members of our church.

7. A public recognition of new members is made in our next weekend service.

ø Follow-Up

1. The prophetic words are recorded onto CDs and transcribed by our staff or volunteers.

2. Copies of the recording and transcription are given to each new member and the pastoral team.

3. An appointment is made for the new members to meet with one of the pastors/leaders and go

over the prophetic words together. This helps the new member understand the meaning of the word and gives us an opportunity to answer any questions they may have for clarification. This also helps the pastor/leader get to know the new member as the Holy Spirit sees them.

4. The pastor/leader prays with the new member.

As a pastor, I've found the prophetic ministry offered in the Affirmation Class to be encouraging and helpful to both the new members and the pastoral team. It is perhaps one of the *best* ways for me to get to know who people really are; the way God sees them. As I learned while getting to know Bill, often what people *do* has very little to do with who they *are* in the Lord's eyes. God's purpose and destiny for each of His children is *far* greater than any of us are able to imagine!

ENDNOTES

Chapter Two

[1] Frank Damazio, *The Prophetic Ministry*, © 1983, Church Life Library, Eugene, Oregon.

[2] ibid.

Special thanks for the writings from Bible Temple in Oregon and the prophetic magazine Proclaim from Springwood Church in Cardiff, Wales, for their helpful resources on the topic of prophetic ministry.

Chapter Three

[1] Eddie Hyatt, *2000 Years of Charismatic Christianity*, © 1996, Eddie Hyatt International Ministries, Inc, P.O. Box 700276, Tulsa, Oklahoma.

[2] John Wimber & Kevin Springer, *Power Evangelism*, © 2009, Regal Books, Gospel Light, Ventura, California.

Chapter Six

[1] Dr. Lawrence Kennedy, *Evangelism Explosion*, © 1970, Tyndale House Publishers, Inc., Carol Stream, Illinois.

[2] Kevin Dedmon, *The Ultimate Treasure Hunt—A Guide to Supernatural Evangelism Through Supernatural Encounters*, © 2007, Destiny Image Publishers, Shippensburg, Pennsylvania.

[3] Bill Leckie, *The Journey*, © 2010, northgatelife publications, Bentonville, Arkansas.

Chapter Ten

[1] Wayne Grudem, *Bible Doctrine*, © 1999, Zondervan Publishing House, Grand Rapids, Michigan.

[2] Donald Gee, *Concerning Spiritual Gifts*, © 1949, Radiant Books, Gospel Publishing House, Springfield, Missouri.

Chapter Twelve

[1] David Blomgren, *Prophetic Gatherings In The Local Church*, © 1979, Bible Temple Inc., Portland, Oregon.

[2] Graham Perrins, *Proclaim!*, © 1993, Published by Springwood Trust, 127 Springwood, Llanedeyrn, Cardiff, Wales.

[3] David Blomgren, *Prophetic Gatherings In The Local Church*, © 1979, Bible Temple Inc., Portland, Oregon.

Chapter Fourteen

[1] Kevin Prosch, *God Is Speaking Through The Music*, © 1993, Jill Prosch, Admin. by Vineyard Music USA.

[2] Graham Perrins, *Proclaim!*, ©, 1993, Published by Springwood Trust, 127 Springwood, Llanedeyrn, Cardiff, Wales.

[3] Laurie Klein, *I Love You, Lord*, © 1978, 1980, 1986, Maranatha Music.

[4] Tamara Winslow, *The Song of The Lord*, © 1996 Kingsway Publications Ltd., P.O. Box 827, BN21 3YJ, England.

[5] Martin Luther, *"Next to the word of God, music deserves the highest praise."*

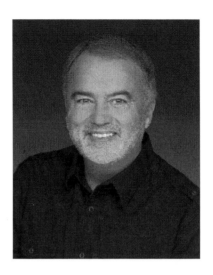

WAYNE DRAIN

Wayne Drain is the Senior Pastor of Fellowship of Christians Church in Russellville, Arkansas. He is a worship leader and songwriter associated with Kingsway/Integrity's ThankYou Music. Being a pastor and a worship leader has given Wayne a unique perspective on team leadership on both the local and international levels. He has been a consultant to a number of churches and ministries across the United States and in countries around the world including South America, Canada, the British Isles, Europe, New Zealand, Singapore and Australia. Wayne has a strong, prophetic gift that comes through in his speaking, worship leading, songwriting and personal ministry. A veteran of many prophetic presbyteries, he feels privileged to move in this encouraging sphere of ministry. Wayne and his wife, June, have three grown children and three grandchildren.

waynedrain.com · foconline.org

TOM LANE

As Executive Senior Pastor of Gateway Church, Tom Lane oversees the church ministries on a weekly basis working with the senior management team to execute the vision and values of the church. Prior to joining Gateway, he served as Senior Pastor of Trinity Fellowship Church in Amarillo, Texas. In addition to his responsibilities at Gateway, Tom also serves on the board of MarriageToday, the non-profit ministry that produces the nationally-broadcast TV program *MarriageToday with Jimmy & Karen Evans*. He is a conference speaker, teacher and church consultant. His relational style and personal experiences bring a warm, tender touch to his leadership, speaking, writing and pastoral ministry. In addition to being the co-author of *He Still Speaks*, Tom is the author of three other books: *The Influence of a Father, Conversations with God* and *Letters from a Dad to a Graduate*. He has also written articles for *Ministry Today* magazine and has produced Foundations—a DVD series on healthy church government. Tom and his wife, Jan, have been married for 40 years. They have four married children and nine grandchildren.

@tlane1002 · gatewaypeople.com

Printed in Great Britain
by Amazon